NORFOLK FLOODS

An Illustrated History of
1912, 1938 & 1953

Neil R. Storey

HALSGROVE

First published in Great Britain in 2012

Title page photograph: *Delivering Bread on Orchard Street, Norwich 27 August 1912*
Contents page: *Boys exploring flooded streets gather around St Margaret's Corner
off Westwick Street during the Norwich Floods, 1912*

British Library Cataloguing-in-Publication Data
A CIP record for this title is available from the British Library

ISBN 978 0 85704 159 3

HALSGROVE
Halsgrove House,
Ryelands Business Park,
Bagley Road, Wellington, Somerset TA21 9PZ
Tel: 01823 653777   Fax: 01823 216796
email: sales@halsgrove.com

Part of the Halsgrove group of companies
Information on all Halsgrove titles is available at: www.halsgrove.com

Printed in China by Everbest Printing Co Ltd

Contents

Dedication:
This book is dedicated to the memory of all who
died in the floods of Norfolk over the years
and is intended as a tribute to all who did so much,
so selflessly in their neighbours' hour of need.

Introduction

From lightning and tempest; from earthquake, fire, and flood;
from plague, pestilence, and famine, Good Lord, deliver us.

The Book of Common Prayer

NORFOLK HAS BEEN no stranger to floods and inundations by the sea down the centuries. The sea is a fickle and cruel mistress, for with one hand she can provide families with a harvest to feed generations and with the crash of a wave or through violent storm; make breach and flood and claim her toll in life along the coast. While further inland if the season is wet and the rain intense enough the rivers and streams of the county, many of which inoffensively flow along through mellow countryside can suddenly become raging torrents powerful enough to plough through bridges, burst and overflow their banks, causing floods, destroying homes and claim yet more lives.

The three floods I cover in this book are some of the most severe to be suffered by the county, not just in the twentieth century but for hundreds of years before. Some of the earliest floods in Norfolk were recorded by Holinshed who, when writing in the sixteenth century, told of a great tide in 1236 that inundated the East Coast damaging ships, sweeping away beaches, demolishing houses, uprooting trees, drowning flocks of sheep and herds of cattle in its wake. Monastic chronicler John of Oxnead wrote of unprecedented flooding at Hickling and Horsey Gap in 1287 when the sea came at night suffocating many in their beds and 'many, when surrounded by the waters, sought a place of refuge by mounting into trees, but benumbed by the cold they were overtaken by the water and fell into it and were drowned.' Norfolk antiquarian Francis Blomefield wrote of an inundation at Norwich in 1290 when the water came down in such abundance the river overflowed St Martin's (Whitefriars) bridge and gates of St Giles' Hospital and 'washed down many houses by its violence.' As you will see in this volume, there are clear parallels to be found between the earliest accounts of floods across Norfolk to the floods in our own time and, I fear, will be found as long as flooding occurs.

Before the floods of 1912, the greatest recorded inundations across the county occurred during what became known as the 'Candlemas Flood' in 1570 when deep snow thawed and drained into the rivers causing 'a great rage of water.' Aggravated by high seas the waters smashed into Lynn and Yarmouth; flood waters spilled over the north of the city and Fye Bridge was washed away. The deepest floods to be recorded in Norwich occurred on 30 November 1614. Known as the 'St Andrew's Flood,' it was claimed the sea penetrated twelve miles inland flooding the city, damaging many churches, houses and places of work. Fortunately no-one was drowned. There would be more floods over the years but the 1912 floods were deeper, more torrential and affected more people than anything the city had seen before or since. In the one hundred years since the floods of 1912 surprisingly little has been published about them. With the centenary of those events in mind I considered it timely to produce an illustrated overview of what happened both in the City of Norwich and across the county of Norfolk based on the accounts published and written in the immediate aftermath of those events.

The Horsey Breach of 1938 is a far lesser known flood but it should not be forgotten. It occurred when an abnormally high and violent tide caused over 500 yards of dunes to collapse and the water poured through flooding 7,500 acres of low-lying hinterland. Fortunately no human lives were lost but many farm and wild animals were drowned. The

Rowing up St Martin's Lane, during the Norwich floods of 1912.

5

Orchard Street during the
Norwich Floods in 1878

impact on the countryside was profound because the sea water flooded into the fresh water of the Broads killing thousands of fish and rendered the farm land it flooded infertile for years after. The 1953 floods are still within very vivid living memory. My chapter revisits the text I first published in my book *Flood Alert: Norfolk 1953* back in 2003 and it is the first time it has been reprinted since then, with some additions and many previously unpublished photographs that have turned up over the years since. When I first began researching the Norfolk floods in the 1990s there were still a few people who had memories from their young childhood in the floods of Norwich and many more who could recall the Horsey breach in 1938 and along the coast in 1953. Although the living memories of 1912 have now passed away it has been my pleasure to meet more people who have shared their memories of the later floods with me as I researched this book and I have had the chance to renew old friendships and contacts but in doing so I sadly note the passing of a number of the contributors to the original volume; among them, my friend Leslie Eaton, a gentleman through and through, and a modest hero in war and peace. He had almost been forgotten as a decorated hero of the 1953 floods. His deeds deserved to be recognised and I am particularly proud to recall them again in this book.

Inevitably, the media compares each flood with the one past and the inundation most recent in the memories of those alive in the city in 1912 were the floods of Monday 18 November 1878. There would be many touchstones in 1912 to revive the memories of those who had lived through the '78 floods, too many. It had been a very wet month and rain gauges at Letheringsett and Costessey had measured six inches of rainfall between the first and the sixteenth day of the month. On the morning of 18 November people were going about their business in the city and attending the market when a few folk arrived with stories of the outlying rivers being swollen and many of their rivulets becoming so engorged with water they had become turbulent steams. Fords that were ordinarily shallow had become impassable and bridges at Worthing, Elsing, Lenwade and a number of other locations had been destroyed. The first alarm in the city came from Carrow Works where the combined streams of the Tas and the upper Yare flow through Lakenham and the Trowse valley joining the Wensum in the Thorpe valley, half a mile below Norwich. The waters were already invading the fields and observers at Carrow saw the waters were likely to rise still higher to invade warehouses and dwellings. The immense volume of water pouring into the Yare was unable to escape to the sea due to a high tide and overflowed across the valley invading a number of houses and cottages and submerged portions of the railway line at Whitlingham and Buckenham.

Rain continued to fall pitilessly with no sign of abatement and by mid-day the violence of the Wensum arrested the attention of everyone crossing the city bridges. The swollen waters of the upper Wensum could not discharge freely through the water gates of the New Mills and at about 3.00pm, as the shades of evening were closing, the waters spilled over and crept swiftly across the marshes onto the Heigham Causeway and on through the courts and alleys in Heigham Street, St Martin-at-Oak and up streets such as Orchard Street, Russell Street, Napier Street and Lothian Street towards Dereham Road. Lives were lost in this area as George Churchyard, a young man employed at William Wills' Tannery on Heigham Street could not make his escape from the premises as the waters rose and was drowned. William Buck, a tailor of Heigham Plain was also claimed by the waters as he tried to wade home and he was carried off by the current along Westwick

Napier Street, Norwich
Floods 1878

Street and into the river, where his body was found some days later.

Through the evening and night the flood spread through St Martin's, St Mary's and St, Michael at Coslany and flooded the extensive beer stores of the Anchor Brewery near St Miles' Bridge. A rapid flowing river, six or seven feet deep, was soon running from Heigham Asylum to St Margaret's Plain; it poured its waters to a distance of two hundred yards up Old Palace Road and half way up Barn Road.

Colegate Street was nearly all under water from the top of Bridge Street to Magdalen Street. On Magdalen Street itself the floods rose on the road, flooding nearby churches, business premises and houses. Bishopgate ran like a stream between the Great Hospital and Bishop's Bridge. Norwich Mayor, Harry Bullard and other gentlemen of the city met at the Guildhall at noon on Tuesday 19 November and resolved to provide coffee, tea and bread for all those in distress at the impromptu refuges that had been established in a number of church school rooms across the city. A Central Committee for the relief effort was established, an immediate order for 2000 loaves of bread was placed and the Home Office was telegraphed for leave to use Government stores.

People trapped in the upper rooms of their houses were evacuated by wagons and carts after climbing from their bedroom windows but only the heaviest of carts or sturdy boats dared enter into the Heigham or Westwick Street areas and many a deed of heroism was performed by worthy citizens, who plunged fearlessly up to their armpits in the muddy waters to help frightened women and children into the boats. The refuges filled up with evacuated people as the afternoon and early evening progressed and a further meeting was held in the Guildhall to source blankets for those who were now homeless. The call was answered decisively with generous donations from the Workhouse, the Barracks, the Castle and a warehouse on Magdalen Street.

At 10.00pm on the evening of Sunday 24 November the waters began to fall and by midnight streets were beginning to clear of water and people began to return to their homes and start making them habitable again. Supplies of wood, coals and coke were placed at the disposal of the relief committee by the railway and gas company and a relief fund that raised thousands was established. Then began the massive effort of clearing up the city and pumping out trapped and lingering waters. The work progressed by day and night, and it was on the night of Monday 25 November that Robert Rudderham, a workman at Carrow would be the final casualty claimed by the flood when he fell off the quayside and was drowned. By the morning of Wednesday 27 November the last of the flood waters had subsided to the marshes.[1] A rare but sadly anonymous handwritten copy of verses rhymes:

Verses on the Norwich Flood 1878

My friends I sing but to bewail
A sad yet most authentic tale
We all have seen with great surprise
The River Wensum's sudden rise
The object of my muse shall be
To induce abundant charity
The citizens have suffered great
The Norwich flood of '78.

For days and weeks the drenching rain
Had spread the water o'er the plain
Till the Wensum oft the sluggard she
Became a deep and dangerous sea
From Costessey Mills to Dereham Road
The waters spreading miles abroad
Seemed bent upon the City Gate
In the Norwich flood of '78

From the Gate House to the Green Hill
The heavy surging waters glide
Devastating each abode
From Gibraltar to Old Palace Road
The unrelenting floods and rain
Filled every house in Tinklers Lane
And Heigham folks bewailed their fate
By the Norwich flood of '78

And now the floods began to flow
Through city district lying low
The poor were forced in wretched plight
From home that cold November night
The mighty waters wheeled around
And swamped St Martin's burial ground
Destitution here was very great
By the Norwich flood of '78

---

1 Author's Note: This account of the Norwich floods of 1878 is based on a contemporary report published by Mark Knights in his rare illustrated book *Norwich Flood, November 18th 1878* (Norwich 1878)

At St Margaret's up each rural court
The waters played with cruel sport
And drove the frantic people out
And washed their chattels all about
The gushing waters inundate
Beds and bedding saturate
Some washed away sad to relate
By the Norwich flood of '78

The whole of Sabbath passed away
And many earnestly did pray
To him who riles the winds and waves
Their little household things to save
At length with Tuesday morning light
The flood diminished in its height
Our suffering to mitigate
In the Norwich flood of '78

And as the waters now recede
Remember those who stand in need
Their flooded homes and cold damp walls
May carry off many souls
May sympathy increase desire
To help the poor with food and fire
'Twas no-one's fault 'twas only fate
The Norwich flood of '78

Let those who live about St Giles
Look down with pity on St Miles
St Mary's, St Swithin's all the three
Are standing 'mongst the misery
Let those who live in luxury
Look down on this calamity
Relieving these from wretched state
By the Norwich flood of '78

God bless the Mayor and upper few
They have proved to be kind hearted men
And publicly subscriptions mete
Assisting each afflicted street
Such actions bounding to their praise
Will soothe and guild these future days
By a knowledge of these duties
Great in the Norwich flood of '78

I hope this book will provide many stories that will provoke pause for thought and cause to remember in equal measure: the consequences, the loss of life, the humanity and kindness shown during the great floods of Norfolk.

Neil R. Storey
Norfolk
2012

The view from Carrow Bridge, Norwich Floods 1878

The Great Flood of 1912

THE CITY AND THE FLOOD

THE MONTH OF AUGUST 1912 had already proved to be a very wet one over the East of England. Rain began falling during the night of 22 August and continued unabated until about mid-day on Saturday 24 August. A depression of considerable intensity and size had caused heavy rain to fall across Ireland, Wales and England. At 7am on Friday 23 August the core of the depression was west of Ireland and had made its progression to over Lancashire by 6pm. The barometric gradient grew rather steep over Ireland and England and high winds from the south west blew over nearly all parts of the coast, while on the extreme northern point of Ireland a gale from the east was experienced. Another cyclonic system of considerable intensity lay stationary over the Skagerrack and caused strong winds or gales from between east and north or north-west over Denmark and the south of Scandinavia while winds reached forty miles an hour across the English Channel. The rough, rainy conditions extended to all the northern departments of France as well as the Low Countries and the coast of North Germany. Over the whole cyclonic-affected area the temperature was abnormally low for the time of year. In England heavy rains and flooding were experienced in a number of parts of the country, notably in the North where many farmers had to abandon any hope of salvaging their hay crop from the flood waters and extensive flooding occurred while in East Anglia rain fell for over twelve hours in South Lincolnshire amounting to seventy tons per acre and hundreds of crops were left submerged under flood water. Further flooding was reported in Huntingdonshire; rain fell continuously in Peterborough for eight hours and the River Nene rose ten inches and at Alconbury Weston flood waters were three feet deep in the main street. The three main roads leading into Huntingdon were under water, Portholme Aerodrome was transformed into a lake and acres of crops such as hay and corn were ruined, many of them being seen floating down the River Ouse.

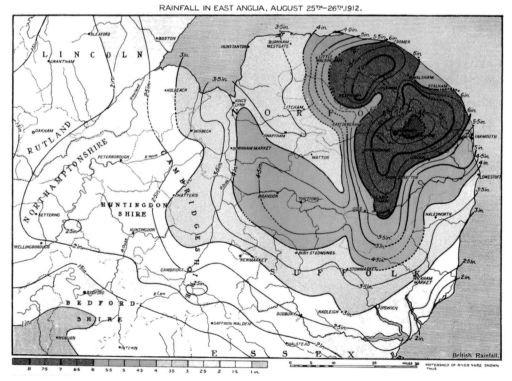

RAINFALL IN EAST ANGLIA, AUGUST 25TH–26TH, 1912.

Metrological map showing the rainfall densities over East Anglia 25-26 August 1912

During the latter part of Saturday the depression moved eastwards to the North Sea and partially dispersed and a clear sky was reported over many parts of the country into Sunday but as the day progressed reports were received from the French and Spanish coasts giving warning of a new cyclonic system developing over the Bay of Biscay with a cloud area soon spreading over our own western and south- western districts and newspapers were already speculating, with just a few days left in the month, that this could well be the wettest August on record.

MONDAY 26 AUGUST

Norfolk had suffered some of the rains of the previous weekend but it was not until about 3.00am on the morning of Monday 26 August 1912 when a gale blew over the county from the north-west and heavy rain began to fall over Norfolk. Norwich and its immediate suburbs were at the centre of the storm and the downpour increased in intensity and 'sheeted down' through the following day and night. To the howling of the gale was added the continual hiss of the falling rain; anyone attempting to go out in it was soon drenched umbrellas were hopeless and the precipitation seemed to penetrate any mackintosh or waterproof garment. By the middle of the day no main line trains could get out of the stations, no mails could arrive and the midday mails could not depart. Trains also failed to get through from the Cromer, Yarmouth and Lowestoft branches causing stranded passengers to be accommodated in the waiting rooms.

Over six inches of rain fell in a continuous downpour over twelve hours amidst a violent gale. Hugh Robert Mill DSc., Director of the British Rainfall Organization stated in his paper for the Royal Meteorological Society, during twenty-four hours the rainfall reached 8.11 inches in some places over an area of 18 square miles over Norwich and its surrounding area. Arthur Preston of Christchurch Lodge, Norwich recorded the rainfall in his garden on 26 August as:

4am-9am: 1.03 inches
9am – 6pm: 5.56 inches
6pm – 9pm: 0.75 inches
Total............ 7.34 inches

At Sprowston weather station the rainfall was recorded as 7.5 inches during the storm; to put this into context, the previous record there for twenty-four hours (9am-9pm) was two inches, during the Norwich floods in 1879. The wettest month recorded prior to 1912 was in October 1892 when rainfall of 7.52 inches recorded *over twenty-eight days*. Norwich had suffered the equivalent of a heavy month's rain fall in just twenty four hours. The mean rainfall over the entire county during the past twenty four hours was 5.08 inches, the total volume of rainfall reckoned to equal to 150,242 gallons; the total weight being 670,720,000 tons.

Rivers swelled, some overflowed while other broke their banks and extensive flooding occurred across the low lying areas of East Anglia sweeping away acres of corn, smashing through bridges, rendering roads impassable and causing extensive damage to homes , shops, factories and buildings. In Norwich the usually placid rivers of the Yare and the Wensum had become raging torrents that burst and spilled over their banks, pouring onto the streets, plains, fields, gardens and homes of the city and the surrounding area.

One of the earliest incidents of the Norwich floods of 1912 occurred on the afternoon of Monday 26 August when the entire front and side of a house collapsed on Churchill Road. The first intimation of the approaching disaster was observed by a young lady in a room at the rear of Mrs. H. Bett's grocery stores on the corner of the road. She was seated in one of the rooms reading when one of the walls began to bulge. Rushing into the road she gave the alarm and it was then seen that the back of the house had broken away from the main building and that the walls were several inches out of perpendicular. At the passage that separates Mrs Bett's premises from the first house on Churchill Road a further, more severe subsidence occurred a few minutes later. The sole occupant of the house at the time was Mrs Florence Meadows, the wife of the owner; she was crossing the upstairs landing when, without any warning, the side of the house collapsed and a huge volume of water shot up into the air at the same time, leading some people at the time to believe the collapse was due to the bursting of a sewer.

Fortunately Mrs Meadows was unharmed but she had scarcely recovered from this shock when the front of her house collapsed. Fortunately the roof of the house retained its position and Mrs Meadows escaped without injury. The walls of the next two houses cracked and the roofs were tilted out of the horizontal to such an extent that it was deemed advisable to the occupants, together with those of the fourth house, to vacate their homes. A portion of road surface also collapsed in the centre of Churchill Road to a depth of several feet and during the rest of the day the authorities were engaged in pumping huge quantities of water out of the hole. The paths on both sides also subsided and for some distance higher up the road was cracked and the kerbs twisted. Three houses at the junction of Sprowston Road and Magdalen Road were also affected by subsidence.

The first casualty of the Norwich floods of 1912. Flood waters underground cause subsidence and bring about the collapse of the front and side of the home of Walter and Florence Meadows at 3, Churchill Road on the afternoon of Monday 26 August 1912.

Later, in the evening a huge tree fell on St Catherine's Plain, breaking through a high wall and stretched itself across the road. From the Norwich City Pumping Station the waters extended to the foot of the uplands at Crown Point. In the other directions, towards and beyond Lakenham the flood was equally extensive, the waters of the Tas mingling with the waters of the Yare. The torrent passing from this latter direction and swirling towards the bridges at Trowse carried an enormous pressure, which the bridge could not withstand. The central arch of the bridge fortunately remained intact, although blocked to some extent by the debris, so that space was afforded for the passage of water, which rushed through at a great rate to the very top of the span. Several yards of parapet and road on the Lakenham side fell into the engorged river and cracks appeared over the remaining structure. A police officer was then put on duty and the bridge was closed to all but very light vehicular traffic even the early morning milk cart had to unload at the church and each can was carried separately over the bridge, even pedestrians were hurried over.

The fall of Lakenham Bridge that spans the river Yare just outside the city occurred at about 9.00pm. Mr Joseph Browne of Vauxhall Street related how he had a narrow escape from disaster here. Having walked from Shotesham, when Browne was near the Caister turning, he was given a lift by a in a trap by Mr Allen, a coachman. The night was pitch dark and when they were about ten yards from the bridge the horse shied. Both Browne and Allen got out of the trap to investigate what had disturbed the horse so and discovered, to their horror, the centre of the bridge had been washed away! The escape was made all the more remarkable for Allen who had driven over the bridge just twenty minutes earlier. Later examination of the structure of the bridge by engineers concluded its collapse was due to the undermining of the pier by the torrents of water, when this was gone the adjoining railway bridge was also weakened and the side was torn out of some nearby railway cottages.

Below left: The extent of the destruction at Lakenham Bridge is revealed after the waters abated.

Below right: Evacuating furniture and possessions by raft from the badly damaged railway worker's cottages near Lakenham railway bridge.

TUESDAY 27 AUGUST

The flood waters continued to rise throughout Tuesday 27 August and district by district, street by street, the deluge came to home after home. As the waters from the upper reaches of the city and streamed down to lower lying areas street gullies had became blocked by the inrush of the waters, which were unable to escape into the overflowing surface drains, basements in riverside areas flooded and many people were driven to the upper floors of their houses seeking refuge from the rising flood waters. Those looking out of upstairs bedroom windows would be met by the sight of grief stricken faces of men and women, and the air filled by the piteous wailing of frightened and confused children. The downstairs rooms of hundreds of homes of hundreds of homes were full of water, almost to the ceiling. Many thoroughfares were under water and quite impassable. Roundsmen tried to carry on but road traffic was almost entirely suspended, the riverside factories closed early followed by just about every other business and the city came to a standstill.

The dire effects of the floods were only too apparent as all railway, telegraphic and telephonic communications between the city and the outside world were cut off as the rain softened the ground and the howling winds and flood made rails unstable or impassable and brought down poles and wires. The telegraphic authorities, however, would not be beaten and arranged for messages to be wired to the nearest centre that was still in working order, at Wisbech in Cambridgeshire and organised a service of motor-cars and motor-cycles to convey the messages to and from Norwich. The city's tramways were entirely stopped early in the evening owing to the depth of water on the main streets and all but two of the dynamos were stopped at the electric lighting station. At 9pm the electric light supply ceased and the greater part of the city was plunged into darkness.

At 6.00am the river had overflowed swirling into the gardens of cottages in the low-lying part of St Martin's uprooting plants and carried off large quantities of soil. Flood waters reached the M&GN City Station end of Heigham Street by 11.00am. The water was soon two feet deep and was rapidly rising and contiguous streets soon became flooded; Napier Street, Exeter Street and Cardigan Street were flooded at the river end while Derby Street became a raging torrent. Groups of spectators stood on the margin of the flood and were continually being driven backwards as the waters rose. A butcher or a baker's boy occasionally tried to cycle a few yards in the water to visit some customer and ultimately came off with a splash. Two girls riding astride their horses took their mounts through some of the streets where the water was not too deep and the occasional wagon on business started to go into the flooded district would rapidly acquire a much larger crew than the driver desired. Groups of men, women and children stood aghast watching the gradual rise of the water unable to get to their homes. Men with trousers rolled up waded through the floods and fetched their children one by one to the higher ground while others visited

Heigham Street, penetrated by some of the first flood waters in the city during the 1912 floods.

their hen houses and moved their poultry to sheds away from the flooded area and soon people were vacating the lower rooms to the upper floors of their houses.

Carts and wagons were making journeys into the flood and removing whole families with some of their treasured belongings. Some of the ensuing scenes were piteous. The people of the Heigham Street area may have been a bit 'hard up' but what they had they had worked hard for and took pride in, keeping the house presentable, scrubbing grates and making sure the front door step was clean and to see all this destroyed by the unstoppable flood waters housewives and mothers fairly broke down and wept; some of them leaving their little homes to take refuge in the Dereham Road National School.

By lunchtime the water had risen to the degree that Barn Road became impassable and stopped the Aylsham Road trams. There will always be those who bring light in disaster; older children made boats of boxes and rafts box lids and went sailing down the streets they usually walked and played on while in the early afternoon Mr George Caso gave a brief exhibition of swimming with breast and over arm strokes and floated for a brief period on Heigham Street.

Traffic over a number of the city's bridges was suspended as the raging torrent of water tore under them and provoked fears for their stability. Pedestrians, including many children, were already unable to proceed up some roads; men who had left their homes and walked through puddles to work were returning at lunch time to find their approach cut off by a quarter of a mile or so of flooded street with water at least two of three feet deep.

Above left: Seen here the waters are calm but at its height the flood water on Derby Street was described as 'a raging torrent.'

Above right: Barn Road, Norwich 27 August 1912.

Above: One for the record. 'Professor' Caso swimming up Heigham Street.

Left: Heigham Street in full flood with 'Professor' George Caso in his swimming trunks.

Above left: Midland & Great Northern Railway, Norwich City Station.

Above right: Mill Yard, St Martin's, Norwich

People began to crowd onto pavements but fortunately some burly corporation workmen were willing to carry women to their homes, much to the intrigue and amusement of the crowds that had gathered at the water's edge. Soon Corporation vans were driven out and women and children loaded up in batches and taken to their respective homes and Mr. Arnold H. Miller, the Town Clerk and Road Foreman, Mr. H. Stratford donned water boots and undertook a survey of the flooded area and did what they could to alleviate disasters caused by the waters.

From the bridge to the right of the M&GN City Station an amazing scene presented itself both up and down the river with the water forced its way through the bridge at a terrific rate bursting warehouse doors and finding its way into every nook and corner of the ground floor of the houses in the immediate neighbourhood. Boats were torn from their moorings and swirled away in the outrush only being stopped by bridges and obstacles further down, one large boat had been overturned and stuck fast for a while until she sank. Oak Street to New Mills was also filling with water and at the New Mills Bridge the swirl of the water was enormous and it was almost impossible to keep the boats safely moored. In every street in the neighbourhood were to be seen men from the electricity and other works bailing out surface water from the manholes.

Oak Street, Norwich

Barrack Street, Norwich

In the neighbourhood of Fye Bridge the river had also overflowed and risen so high barges moored alongside were level with the road. Men in Messrs. Allen's warehouse were stranded and the New Star pub had no customers because no boats were available with which to reach the bar of the house. It was impossible to get through Fishergate on foot and opposite St Edmund's Church there was a very large pool.

Every yard on the river side of Barrack Street was knee deep in water and the inconveniences and suffering occasioned by it to the poor residents of the neighbourhood was most pitiful. In others concerns were raised for elderly people in Palace Yard who could not be moved but they managed to get to their top rooms. Opposite the Barracks large tracts of gardens teeming with vegetables only apple trees could be seen above the water and all hoardings had been cleared of their picturesque lettering by the torrential downpour.

The waters rose a few feet around the base of Cow Tower and wherries were straining at their mooring as they floated over what had until recently been river bank and path. It was observed there that a mooring post that normally stood about nine feet out of the water here, only about a foot was still visible above the flood and a number of boathouses were almost submerged, while meadows and the recreation ground of the King Edward VI School had become a lake. In a number of places the waters almost reached Riverside Road from the river while the waters had reached half-way up the walls of Pull's Ferry.

Crowds gather on Quayside near Fye Bridge to watch the flood waters

Concerns were also raised for the fate of many historic buildings and churches in the city including the cathedral as the waters came over the banks of the river reinstating part of the old waterway through Pull's Ferry, spreading past Cow Tower, across the King Edward VI School field to past the pavilion, onto the walk surrounding the Garth, across the cathedral close garden and entered the cloisters.

The inhabitants of Prince of Wales Road began to feel the effects of the flood from about mid-day and were engaged in erecting various safeguards against its encroachment. In the dip near Foundry Bridge both paths were rapidly rendered impassable for foot passengers and the water gradually spread along the newly built Recorder Road along with a number of neighbouring streets. Very soon the timber in the nearby Messrs. Porter & Son's yard was afloat and Messrs. Morris & Co's garage was completely flooded. Near Foundry Bridge the river had covered the tow path and it was impossible to state whether the pleasure steamer Jenny Lind was on the path or still in the river. The houses known as Foundry Bridge Buildings were as flooded as the rest and it was impossible to reach the doors, here the water had crept at least 12ft up the lane in two hours. It seemed as if from every upstairs an inhabitant's head protruded, many of them bemoaning the fact they had 'lost their breakfast' because of the flood. The water from the river had risen considerably in every yard and lane off King Street and across to Thorpe Station where it looked like an expansive stream.

The historic Cow Tower surrounded by flood and wherries straining at their moorings as they are carried by the flood over river bank and path.

The view across the flooded King's School field from Lollards Road off Riverside.

Rowing past Pull's Ferry, Norwich.

Crowds fills the paths and the traffic carries on despite the flooding on Prince of Wales Road, Norwich.

The junction of Prince of Wales Road and Rose Lane (left).

The view from foundry bridge showing part of Thorpe Station and the SS *Jenny Lind* floated on the overflowing river waters over the towpath, Norwich.

The horse and cart fromThe British Gas Light Company Ltd making headway up flooded Bishopgate, Norwich.

The flooding extended from Thorpe Station to Carrow where houseboats, yachts and a number of smaller craft had come adrift from their moorings and were simply drifting about, some of them on a most dangerous condition. The flood waters spread from Carrow Road to Hardy Road preventing employees of Laurence & Scott starting work. At the Carrow Works the water invaded the cellars destroying a large quantity of starch. Dynamos were inundated and the various departments were deprived of electric lights and power.

The floods at Carrow, Norwich, 27 August 1912

Below left: Carrow Road, Norwich.

Below right: Laurence & Scott's works on Hardy Road, Norwich.

Grave fears were aroused among the population that even more properties would succumb to the after effects of the deluge. Anxious crowds began to cluster on every bridge through which the waters were racing with the rapidity of a Niagara torrent but fortunately the police exercised the wise precaution of moving people on who tried to linger too long on the parapets. At the Anchor Brewery the cellars filled with water and beer barrels were seen floating about. In the engineer's and fitter's shop there was four feet of water submerging the lathes and motors. On the opposite side of the river the works of Messrs. Barnards Ltd were in similar trouble where they had as much as eight feet of water in their cellars. At St George's the *Norwich Mercury* printing works the basement was awash, the boilers under water and dozens of bales of paper afloat, the lower rooms of the Technical School were also flooded as were Howlett and White and other firms nearby who suffered from the effects of the rising and torrential waters of the River Wensum. St George's Bridge was an observation point for huge throngs for here the swirl of the waters could be seen to the fullest advantage. Throughout the day the debris of yards and factories higher up the river steamed down in an unending succession such incongruous items as butcher's blocks, dog kennels, garden palings, brewer's tubs and countless numbers of corks and barrels were all carried along the swirling torrent smashing into bridge after bridge, then into the mid-stream and sent on its way towards Yarmouth. The remains of a baker's shop, huge boards, shelves, loaves of bread, even the baker's kneeding trough with his baker's apron still hanging on the side were also seen floating by. These latter items had come from the roller mills of R. J. Read that fronted Westwick Street and backed onto the river where a wall collapsed under the pressure of the swollen waters. The premises suffered an invasion from an enormous volume of water that left the boiler house under nine feet of water, ruined sacks of meal and flour and caused tools and implements to float about. It was only by the most strenuous efforts that the horses in the stables were saved from drowning. Also swept away was a considerable portion of the model bakery that had Read's had set to supply 24,000 loaves daily to the army for the duration of the manoeuvres taking place in the county at the time.

During the afternoon more subsidence occurred. The gardener at the Catholic Rectory discovered a huge subsidence at the extremity of the garden that extended about 6ft under the adjacent school hall connected with the Unthank Road Baptist Church. The hole was 18ft across and 15ft wide and deep. By 3.30pm the waters were within an inch of the top of the arch of St Miles's Bridge and great fears were expressed for its safety. The bridge was not lost but an old prophesy relating to the previous bridge held true. The bridge was said to bear a carving of a dragon at the centre point of its arch which prompted the saying 'When the dragon drinks Heigham sinks' and poor Heigham did indeed suffer on this day. The depth of the flood water exceeded all the city's extant flood marks, in Heigham and Pockthorpe the waters were eight feet deep by 11.00pm and had risen to 13ft by 1.00am.

The high flood waters under St Miles' Bridge on the afternoon of 27 August 1912.

During Tuesday evening exciting scenes were witnessed at Bishop Bridge where large quantities of timber had floated down from the wood yards on the right bank of the Wensum above Cow Tower. The work of the men engaged in clearing out the floating lumber drew large crowds keen to observe this unique operation.

All through Tuesday night, in the fitful and eerie light of improvised flares and clusters of candles, which guttered in the wind, a flotilla of boats, every available cart, wagon and even the Corporation dust carts, manned by police and volunteer rescuers, went from house to house in the inundated streets rescuing inhabitants from the upper stories of their homes. Despite assurances that all would be well and that rescue parties would return for those left behind most refused to go to bed and they kept a weary vigil.

A number of gallant rescues were reported; Mr Louis Tillett, MP for Norwich from 1906 until he stood down at the 1910 election, was the hero of one of the rescue parties. He had gone to a police station to volunteer his services when a man arrived in great distress. His wife was very ill and there was no means of getting a nurse or doctor to her. Mr. Tillett at once procured two nurses and, accompanied by Police Inspector Seaman, started off for the house. Walking along the wall of a wood yard, Mr. Tillett carried one of the nurses while the Inspector carried a ladder. Unfortunately Mr Tillett tore his hand on some wire at the top of a garden wall he had been compelled to scale but he remained atop a shed while Inspector Seaman carried the nurses into the house where the sick woman was lying.

The force of the flood waters is well captured on this photograph of Lothian Street

In Bath House Yard off Oak Street residents whose own houses had been flooded went to the aid of their neighbours who were in danger of drowning. Mr. James Stark and Mr. Warr swam along the yard to the house where a Mrs Brown had been trapped and the two men carried her and her son to safety. Mr. Finch, whose workshop on the river's brink had been ruined by the inundation abandoned his own woes and rowed his boat to several houses and removed the occupants from the upper stories and to the safety of their relatives on Oak Street.

Rescue boat and crewman on Derby Street.

Mr. Sadd carried many people on his back to safety, sometimes wading through water up to his chest. Mr. Sadd and Mr. Edward Carey of Oak Street also helped carrying people to safety, also using their boats, Mr Sadd and Mr Carey laboured in their rescue work for some 21 hours, remaining in their same wet clothes throughout. These brave men evacuated many people from the Oak Street area including thirty people from Fellmonger's Yard along with others from such places as Howman's Yard, Little Queen Caroline Yard, Big Queen Caroline Yard and Rayner's Yard.

Rescue boats on Lothian Street photographed from Barn Road.

Mr. Edward Bullard and Mr Porritt, the fish merchant had a narrow escape on Westwick Street. They had set out in a boat to help evacuate their neighbours when they were drawn by the current into the yard of R. J. Read's roller mills and were fortunately held by against a submerged muck wagon, had they not have been stopped both they and their little boat could have been carried into the river which was at that time 'raging like the sea' and they would have almost certainly been capsized.

Mr R. J. Read jnr. stripped off to his undergarments on one of the upper stories of the mill, grabbed a rope and swam across Westwick Street to a cottage while his friend Lord Wodehouse took the other end and helped him set up a pulley arrangement and by this means food contributed by Mr Read and Mr William Snelling was passed to scores of hungry and frightened people.

There were also some lucky escapes. The Secretary of the YMCA had been busy making arrangements to rescue the homeless and destitute when a telephone message was received from the City Engineer, asking for volunteers to man a boat and assist in rescuing people, he recalled:

The response was instantaneous. Four of us hurried down to Oak Street and found Superintendent Hedges with a boat ready. After great difficulty we got our craft to Heigham Street. The people in one of the yards were clamouring to be rescued, and one of the boats overturned, throwing its occupants into about 10ft of water. We were able to save a number of people but could not deal with one fourth of those who cried to be taken away. The distress of women and children was most pathetic and moved some of us to tears. One of our party had a very narrow escape. He had just taken an old blind women, eighty-four years of age, from a bedroom, when the ladder gave way and he and his burden were only saved by the ladder crashing into a down stair window frame.

Another boat containing eighteen or twenty women and children was being taken from Globe Yard in Heigham Street to a point at which they could be landed for shelter. In the lower part of Orchard Street the boatman lost his bearings by a point or two when it became impaled upon the spikes of some partially submerged garden railings. At once the boat began to fill with water and there were shrieks of anguish for the depth of water there was very deep. Fortunately another boat was within hailing distance, drew alongside and not without considerable difficulty a transfer of passengers was made, the last one was hardly out when the boat had filled up and promptly sunk.

Outside the Heigham Causeway Tavern, Miss F. Norton, the landlord's daughter, was being lowered from a bedroom into a boat when it capsized and the occupants were thrown into the water. A policeman who had been in the boat with her held the girl above the water and her father seeing his daughter's peril, lowered a blanket which she managed to grab hold of and was hauled back up to her room. In another incident a dying woman was removed safely and with tenderness from Midland Street to the workhouse infirmary.

Some were far less fortunate, poor Mrs Kemp had been terrified by the coming of the flood waters and had died from fright and shock on removal from Goat Yard on Oak Street. One of the most tragic deaths was that of a four month old infant, the son of Edward Charles Poll of 13, Canterbury Place, North Heigham. Boats had been commandeered for rescue work, the flood stream here was running fiercely and Mr Poll was engaged rescuing his family from the upper windows of their flooded home. He had already got an older child to a place of safety and had returned for his wife and the younger children. They were safely got into the boat but their little vessel was carried by the force of the current onto some garden railings where it was upset and the occupants thrown into the water. In the struggle to save themselves the mother, who had been holding a child under each arm, lost her hold of the infant which was swept away and drowned.

A model statue of George Brodie, hero of the Norwich Floods.

George Brodie (46), a well-known fish porter of the Norwich Fish Market set off from his home at Saw Mills Yard to help with the flood rescue efforts at the height of the floods on Tuesday 27 August when, during the evening, he lost his foothold and was swept away. His body was discovered floating in the water near Bullard's Wharf, St Miles, the following morning at an inquest held at the Norwich coroner's court Brodie's widow related how George came home to leave his coat after being engaged in rescue work for four hours. She tried to persuade him to remain indoors but he replied 'There are some dear little children who want getting out. I am going back again. I will get them out but I shall not be very long before I am home.' The widow added, sadly, 'I never saw him again.'

Rescue work was also rendered difficult by those who would not leave their houses, declining any offer of help until the waters had risen to the level of the bedroom windows, at which point they rushed to the sills and hung out screaming for help. Many heartrending scenes were witnessed during the nights on these streets as women and children huddled together praying and singing hymns. Rescue efforts continued into the daylight of Wednesday 28 August as the waters failed to abate as quickly as hoped after some abnormally high tides at the mouth of the Yare at Great Yarmouth held up the dissipation of the flood

---

FIRE AND FLOOD

On Tuesday afternoon the city fire brigade were engaged in pumping out water from Messrs. Howlett and White's cellars when they received and urgent call to the electric light works as the dynamos were threatened by the incoming wash of water. Despite the energetic work of the men the place was flooded and the light cut off. From there the engine was taken to the Gas Works on Palace Plain, where the boiler house was flooded.

A fire broke out on Tuesday evening in the gas generating department at Thorpe Station and inflammable materials ignited and caused a large blaze. The motor-fire engine and the city brigade went there, accompanied by the Chief Constable. After an hours' hard work the firemen succeeded in extinguishing it.

A small fire that might have resulted in a serious conflagration, broke out at Messrs. Robert Ruymp and Son's premises in St George Street on Wednesday morning after flood water reached a quantity of lime. Help was sought and a detachment of soldiers from 16th Lancers arrived; at one point the fire looked as if it might spread to Porter's timber stores but fortunately this was averted the flames were extinguished. The soldiers then remained on the premises to manhandle the lime bags into a safer place to prevent further outbreak.

WEDNESDAY 28 AUGUST

Part of the vast flood plain around Norwich viewed from Drayton Road.

Another view showing more of the flooding viewed from Drayton Road.

With the dawn came a chance to view the extent of the unprecedented flood waters. Never in the history of the ancient city had such scenes been witnessed as those which took place during those few days. Standing on the terrace of the old castle, high above the city one was able to look over a vast expanse of waters, which stretched away into the far distance. The valley of the river above the New Mills gave the appearance of one great lake and from Drayton Road water of a curiously creamy colour extended as far as the eye could seen. The approach to The Dolphin footbridge was completely submerged and the upper portion, which rises by a sharp incline, was alone visible.

Flooding on the street by the Swan Laundry, Heigham, Norwich.

On the roadway outside the gates of the Swan Laundry and Baths the river had swollen to a tremendous width. Mr Ransome, the lessee, had to drag his piano upstairs during the morning and rescue what other household furniture he could; by the afternoon there were four or five feet of water in his residence, the waters reaching almost to the troughs of the bath roof. In the adjacent laundry work for the one hundred and twenty hands was at a standstill. One of the boilers had been stopped by water on Monday, the second followed on Tuesday when the water rose to four feet and completely covered the flues.

From vantage points near the Gate House pub on Dereham Road another great expanse of water could be viewed like some great panoramic lake that stretched in length from the city to Hellesdon and in breadth from Dereham Road to Drayton Road. Its volume submerging kitchen gardens, summer and boat houses, allotments and numerous tomato houses full of fruit just ripening.

At Trowse there were acres of water to the right and left of the wrecked bridge, Trowse Church and Parish Rooms were under three feet of water and many gravestones were washed out of position. Locals were to recall how the old church stood out like a 'flinten fortress' standing in the centre of a vast moat stretching to White Horse Lane and the Common while the roads around ran like a wide stream. Towards Lakenham, the Baths were completely surrounded and in some of the cottages nearby there was three feet of water. Garden crops were destroyed, pig sties were wrecked and here and there was the dead body of a drowned pig; Lakenham Cock was surrounded by water.

The torrents of water still pressing against Trowse bridge.

The receded flood waters reveal the damage inflicted upon Trowse Bridge.

Norwich Floods, August 27/12. Trowse Bridge.   No. J. & S. 778

Above left: Trowse church suffered flooding to a depth of 3ft of water but still it stood like a ' flinten fortress standing in the centre of a vast moat.'

Above right: Flooding near the Cock public house, Lakenham.

Left: Russell Street and St Barnabas Church, North Heigham, Norwich.

The lower lying areas of housing in Norwich, Pockthorpe and Heigham, much of it inhabited by some of the poorer people of the city suffered the severest flooding. It was estimated some ten thousand of these people were driven from their homes or had to be rescued from their desperate plight, many of them loosing what little they had in the process, notable among the losses were the thousands of canaries that drowned. Mr R. Roll, Secretary of the Alliance Cage Bird Society, stated that the floods had 'caused ruinous losses to canary fanciers in Norwich.' The Heigham district was the centre of the canary breeding industry where many of the city's three thousand breeders were working men who supplemented their earnings as boot and shoe operatives by their sales of the birds they bred. The general practice was to keep the canaries in a specially constructed shed in the back garden hence many of these aviaries were simply swept away by the deluge and scores of cages containing dead birds were seen floating in the streets over the following days. The tragedy was compounded by the hundreds of dead domestic pets and even livestock that had to be left to their fate and ended up floating dead on the flood waters.

Despite the waters receding enough for the GER to repair the line and get their first train in carrying food and perishable goods around a half of the city remained cut off throughout Wednesday apart from access by boat. Some of the lowest areas suffered rising water levels as the higher ground drained away. Thorpe Old Hall, the residence of Major Cubitt, was partly under water while in Thorpe village the river overflowed, boats escaped from their moorings and were damaged or sunk. At the Thorpe Gardens pub water rose to a level of three and a half feet in the bar; the road was a foot deep in places; gravel and stones that had been washed down from the higher gardens extended across the road every few yards while the surrounding fields were reduced to a watery waste in which stacks of hay and corn could be seen floating around.

Those rescued from their flooded homes in the city were taken to temporary shelters established in schools, churches, chapels and public building in the higher portions of Norwich where mattresses were provided courtesy of the Commanding Officers of the 2nd East Anglian Field Ambulance (Bethel Street) and 16th Lancers (then stationed at the Cavalry Barracks), and blankets from Mr George Chamberlin of Chamberlin's Department Store were handed out. Many of the workers who had failed to reach their homes distractedly made the rounds of these temporary shelters endeavouring to find their wives and children.

The rescue effort in the city had been magnificent; seven schools had been immediately opened as refuge centres and with both Mayor and Deputy Mayor away an emergency meeting of the City Council was convened on Wednesday morning with Alderman George Chamberlin in the chair. It was decided to form a relief committee that would take the relief effort in hand. An appeal was immediately issued for subscriptions and was generously supported by people from both the city and from across the county, a fund boosted early on by a subscription of £1,000 from J. and J. Colman. All charitable organisations in the city co-operated well and soon the relief effort reached a good state of organization.

The following is a list of emergency relief centres set up across the city and the numbers of people they fed and gave shelter to during the floods:

St Augustine's School : 600
Bull Close Schools: 500
Dereham Road Methodist School: 500
Dereham Road Baptist School: 200
National School, Dereham Road: 200
Nelson Street School: 200
Wensum View School: 50
Heigham Radical Club: 103
YMCA: 280
Salvation Army: 150
All Hallows Mission: 56
Labour Institute 66
Friend's Meeting House: 89
Messrs. Barnwell's: 50

A total of twelve births occurred in the shelters. It should also be recorded that many people, some of them of limited means, independently opened their homes to flood victims such as an elderly widow on Northumberland Street who gave refuge to a number of flood victims denying herself the necessities of life to help strangers. Every house cut off by water, about 1,100 homes, was visited by a relief party and supplied with food and other necessaries by the Corporation carts. When reached some had eaten nothing for over twenty four hours, the problem not only being the height and flow of the flood waters but the fact that the delivery of relief was hindered because many families lived in courts and yards to which access cannot be gained in carts or boats instead a hardy relief agent would have to plunge several feet into water to deliver the rations by hand.

Each stranded household received a twenty-four hour food ration for each occupant containing half a pint of milk, half a pound of pressed beef, quarter pound chocolate bars and a two pound loaf along with one box of matches and two candles; those below the flood level were also delivered fresh water. The rounds were made as frequently as possible, not only to maintain the supply of food and emergency requirements but also to keep an eye out for settlement and subsidence in the flooded properties and on the roads. Rescue workers in the Heigham area were surprised that many of those who had taken to their upper bedrooms in the midst of the flood first requested fresh water; truly, as in the lines of Coleridge's Rime of the Ancient Mariner there was 'Water, water every where, Nor any drop to drink.' Supplies were quickly obtained and by means of bottles, poles and string were supplied to those in need.

Wednesday was a day for further reckoning; buildings were still collapsing under the torrents of water or having been weakened by the flood. The most serious collapse in the city was at the three storey Printing Works of the *Norwich Mercury* that stood on the banks of the river at St George's Bridge. The foundations had been undermined by the water to a considerable distance back from the river so that it was impossible to shore the building above. The whole front of the two lower stories was torn away and the remainder of the premises, with a tall tower and chimneys above, was threatened with disaster. The large bundles of old newspapers that were stored on the ground floor, were all swept away by the rushing water. The second floor consisted of the smith's shop, foundry, machine room and binding room together with the photographic department was also damaged and one of the coppers from the stereotyping department was carried away into the river. Men were still at work in the various departments when the alarm was given that parts of the building were collapsing. The adjoining building, a malt-house occupied by Messrs Bullard & Son was also undermined and extensively damaged. On the other side of the river a building owned by F. W. Harmer the clothing manufacturer also collapsed and the gable end of the Boston Blacking Co. fell into the river.

The torrents of the River Wensum in flood caused this collapse at *The Norwich Mercury* printing works at St George's, Norwich.

The Boston Blacking Company's premises at St George's after partial collapse into the river.

In several other parts of the city the waters had permeated underground and undermined several properties and roads cracking walls and causing them to tilt at alarming angles or even collapse. At one house on Portersfield Road the bay window collapsed and at many places, both in that thoroughfare and in Whitehall Road, paths and palings sunk several inches. The gable of a house at the end of Whitehall Road was split from top to bottom.

The water company issued a notice to the public requesting that great care should be taken in the use of the city supply of drinking water as the flood had put out the fires of the pumping engine boilers in the pumping station and the supply depended upon the surface reservoirs, which only contained sufficient for about two days. Fortunately the flood waters did not rise above the level of the clean waters wells. The appearance on the streets on Wednesday night was extraordinary. There were no electric street lamps alight and in many shops the chief method of illumination was by candles placed in bottles.

Westwick Street became a river during the Norwich floods.

Opposite: Coslany Street looking towards St Miles' Bridge.

A newspaper reporter had been to visit the Westwick Street and Heigham Street area chanced upon boatman William John Marrison of Fox and Goose Yard off St Martin's Lane, who had been engaged in rescue work throughout Tuesday from eleven in the morning until eleven at night and had brought over a hundred people to safety (including Mr and Mrs Poll and their older child). Marrison had been joined in his rescue work by PC Horner. They told him of their exploits carrying over a hundred people to safety but at about one in the morning on that Wednesday night their boat was capsized and they were plunged into the seething waters. PC Horner managed to swim to a wall and clamber over to a place of safety; Marrison managed to extricate himself from the water too but neither saw each other get out. The Constable promptly went to his police station to report Marrison as drowned but was delighted to be proved wrong half an hour later when his compatriot in rescue came to the police station to report the loss of PC Horner!

On Wednesday night the special correspondent of *The Times* reported:

The floods reached their height this morning and since then the water has steadily fallen. The great city is, nevertheless, in a deplorable plight. It is estimated one square mile of streets is flooded...Tonight the people are looking anxiously at the sky. Heavy clouds rolled up after a brilliant morning, and now there seems to be every prospect of another downpour before the night is out. Indeed, just before I started to telegraph there was a sharp shower. Ten thousand people are either homeless of living in the upper floors of Norwich houses through the floods. Some of them are being cared for by friends and others are being accommodated in the public elementary schools.

The chief thoroughfares are in darkness; the post office, hotels and many of the business houses are lighted by lamps and candles and some of the places of amusement are closed through want of electric light. No train succeeded in getting out of or into the Great Eastern terminus today, but an attempt is to be made to run the up-mail train tonight...The station yard is filled with carriages, cabs, wagonettes and motor-cars ready to drive people into Norwich. The GER are also running a special wagonette service for passengers to and from Norwich and the railway ticket is available by that. The railway station at Norwich is deserted except for the arrival and departure of conveyances plying between the city and more fortunate places over the water. Everybody and everything has to take to the road and I passed on the way from Wymondham this afternoon; passengers, mails, luggage and perishable merchandise. The road was crowded; it actually became congested here and there. Every sort of vehicle, old and new, has been pressed into use and famine prices are being paid in the district for horse and motor conveyances.

THE PERSONAL REMINISCENCES OF A RELIEF WORKER

Many of those involved in relief work did so without any previous training and in the face and immediate aftermath of the floods acted on their wits and wish to help their fellow Norwich citizens; this is the story of one of them, told in his own words:

It occurred to me that just across the road was a large school building. Selecting several children, who were very wet, I sent them across to the schools, the doors of which I found open and soon the good caretaker was trying to comfort the frightened little ones. After arranging for fires to be lighted in the schools upstairs and down, I went and purchased biscuits, tea, sugar, butter, bread and milk, whilst the caretaker and her daughter put water on and made some tea and coffee, which was given to each person as they arrived, wet and cold. About an hour after this several fresh helpers arrived on the scene of action and the people were helped out of their wet clothes and placed in front of large fires and this with the hot drinks went a long way, in my opinion, to warding off serious illness and even death itself. Only those who saw the dreadful condition of some of the people as they arrived, straight out of the water in some instances, can fully realise the necessity for hot drinks and fires at such a time.

One thing I would like to do at this point is to bear personal testimony to the goodness of God in answering a prayer for aid. Following a hurried prayer for help and money came a direct answer, for an unknown lady came to me in the street and slipped a piece of gold (£1) into my hand and soon afterwards another pound was given by a gentleman and thus we were helped out of one of the greatest difficulties at the time

By the kindness of both strangers and friends we were able to purchase enough necessities to keep going till official relief was forthcoming. The Guardians sent a supply of food, hot drinks and blankets shortly after 9pm; all these were very welcome and were soon put to the best advantage. Just at this time, to add to the terror and confusion of the scene, the electric light failed, but the helpers did not lose their presence of mind and very soon the rooms were lighted by gas and candles.

The scenes at this time in the shelter were and always must remain indescribable, as the sights seen by the helpers that night are too terrible to place on record or even mention. Up till midnight the boats were constantly bringing loads of people who had been rescued from the flooded houses across to the shelters to be taken care of.

Magdalen Street during the Norwich floods.

At midnight some of the helpers went home to bed for two hours. A supply of porridge was prepared and was taken down to the shelter, where several men having also snatched two hours' rest were waiting for something hot before starting rescue

Above left: Magdalen Street filled with carts taking people on tours of the flooded streets of Norwich for a penny a time.
Above right: One of the carts transporting city folks through the floods on Heigham Street.

People sitting out the floods in their upper rooms on Carrow Road.

Still serving, 'business as usual' at The Causeway Tavern on the corner of Russell Street.

work again. The hot porridge was eagerly devoured by them and when they had gone I went to see if any more people had been rescued and found several men, women and children just being brought in by the boats from the houses; having been without food since mid-day Thursday, they were almost famished. Directly they arrived, however, something hot was given to them and they in turn were placed around the still blazing fire.

Never shall I forget the early morning sunrise of Wednesday 28 August. I was very cold and sharp but bright, like an early winter's morning and one had to rub one's eyes to wonder if it was all a dream but the wonderment received a rude awakening for on entering the shelter there were between 300 and 400 people then being cared for.   Messrs. Caley generously supplied large quantities of hot cocoa and Messrs. Bullard and Sons also sent round coffee. With the coming of the dawn also came fresh supplies of hot tea and coffee, bread, butter and milk from the Guardians and all the rescued people had an ample breakfast and some good advice was given to the about not going back to their homes until they were told to do so.

As the second day drew to a close the organisation of the relief was more systematically carried out and it was no longer necessary to rely upon voluntary money to supply the people's bodily needs. During the evening songs, music and gramophone selections were given by several contributors to the delight of the younger refugees.

It is interesting to note that although several of the people were in deep distress, yet their faces could relax into smiles at the comic songs that were sung by the helpers, who in some instances had never before sung in public and who were willing to make themselves ridiculous in order to cheer up the homeless people under their charge. After the music had ceased, supper was served, consisting of bread, cheese and cocoa for the adults whilst milk, bananas, bread and butter were given to the children.

Supper being finished a hymn was sung and a short prayer said, and once again the tired-out, homeless people turned in to try and get sleep under what must have been anything but happy conditions. One must here remark, however, upon the real English pluck of these suffering people, who in spite of the terrible ordeal they were passing through, found time to cheer each other up and many a hearty laugh was raised by someone or other offering to 'shake up the feathers' of a neighbour's plank bed. 'Can you keep yourself warm?' was often heard during the night, and if an old person answered no then someone readily offered to give up his or her blanket so that someone older might get to sleep.

The actions of the Royal Army Medical Corps (Territorials), who, on the second night, when blankets were a scarce commodity, willingly gave up their large line overcoats to keep the old men and women warm, was greatly appreciated. One old man entered heartily into the spirit of the joke and many sad hearts and caused roars of laughter when, clad in a soldier's overcoat and hat, he walked down the room saluting and saying, 'Now I am off for a soldier' whereas he was in reality then off to be to sleep in a warm coat whilst the noble fellow who gave up his coat had to shiver outside in the cold until the morning on duty. No words can express the gratitude of all the helpers for the noble gestures of the members of the RAMC. They were invaluable.

Between fresh numbers returned to their homes, although some were hardly fit for habitation, yet who can blame anyone for going back, for 'be it never so humble there's no place like home.' May God Almighty spare the city from such a dreadful disaster again.

Helpers at the Salvation Army Citadel flood refuge centre, Norwich.

THURSDAY 30 AUGUST

The special correspondent for *The Times* reported the situation of the floods in Norwich on the morning of Thursday 30 August:

Rain began to fall heavily again this morning. It came down in a sheet for some hours and did not abate until after noon. It is clear, however, from a tour of the low-lying districts of the city which I have just made that the floods have now done their worst and the situation, bad as it is, cannot again become really acute unless there are torrential rains during the next few days in the high ground from which the Wensum flows into Norwich. I am told that an ordinary rainfall like that of this morning cannot do a great amount of harm.

The flood water level has been falling rapidly since yesterday. The river is quite three feet lower and this morning I walked through several streets for the passage of which I had yesterday to hire a conveyance. Magdalen Street and the land close to the Cathedral is now fairly clear. There is still, however, a great deal of water out at Heigham and hundreds of houses that are still only approachable by carts and boats.

Between 1,000 and 2,000 persons are still being cared for in the rescue centres. Some of the men have left their temporary shelter to man the pumps and make a fire in their drenched cottages but very few of the women and children have ventured to return home although the water has receded from the majority of the flooded houses. I visited this morning the Bull Close Road and St Augustine's Schools, in which accommodation has been found for nearly 1,000 refugees. I saw some sad spectacles and others that were grimly pathetic.

At the Bull Close Road School a little red-haired girl went to the piano and began to play some popular tunes. In an adjoining class room boots were being distributed to the worst shod. The women with their babies sat sad-eyed on the scholars' narrow forms. The men who were left stared moodily before them. They were without both home and work, for the floods have brought many factories to a standstill. A clergyman whom I met in the school told me that at least 5,000 persons had been thrown out of employment in the poorer parts of the city. The children, driven into the schoolroom from the playground by the rain, were as merry as crickets. Three of four hundred people slept in this school last night and still more at St Augustine's. I arrived there soon after the doctor and a moment before a poor woman asked him to go at once to a house in Oak Street in the middle of the flooded area. 'There is a women dying there' she said; it was one of the tragedies of the floods. The scenes were similar to those I had witnessed at the other school. There was despair on some of the older faces but as a whole I was struck by the fine optimism of the human character. The majority were settling themselves down to make the best of a bad job.

And what bad job it is I realised when I plunged down through the driving rain by way of Oak Street to Heigham. Damaged furniture was piled up in the yards at the back

Inside a house wrecked by flood at Heigham, Norwich.

of Oak Street. Shops were being re-opened but chiefly to let the water run away. Women were ripping up oil cloth in front of parlours, while men were pumping water from the basements. It seemed to me that hundreds of houses had been seriously damaged. I found one man sitting over a fire in a room in which there were three feet of water yesterday. The walls were still wet but he was still cheerful and was waiting, pipe in mouth, to welcome his family home. In another house I found a woman sitting disconsolately on a chair in the middle of her upstairs furniture with mops and pails all around.

It was however, at Heigham, where many of the people had no food for more than twenty-four hours, that I found the greatest desolation. I was prepared for it when I crossed the swirling Wensum and saw three wrecked skiffs carried down the stream. The water had fallen considerably, but several roads were still impassable. I could not be surprised at this when I came across a flood mark in New Mill Road, just over the Wensum Bridge. This mark was completely hidden yesterday and the new chalk mark was eighteen inches higher than anything that has been recorded before, although the stone goes back to the year 1614.

Nearby the pumps were at work in closed factories and at an important crossing I had to accept the hospitality of the corporation cart-ferry for a hundred yards. Water was still out to the depth of two feet in some of the neighbouring roads and in Napier Street I saw a policeman in a boat with a rescue ladder resting against an upper window. Still, things were not nearly so serious as they were early yesterday morning when it is said that in some parts the water rose in the houses above ten feet. By tomorrow every street will probably be clear of water and the heavy task of making good the damage can be begun in earnest.

I came across roads broken up by the floods, bridges broken down, walls that had collapsed and a station yard [Norwich City Station] strewn with great tree trunks. Traffic facilities improved greatly in the course of the day. Late last night the up mail was safely run through from Norwich to London. It was the first train to either enter or leave the city since Monday afternoon. A few passenger trains were got away to the South and the west this morning but there is still no railway communication with the Norfolk coast of the Broads. The tramway service was resumed during the morning, after two days complete suspension. There is a great delay by telegraph and telephone. Both services were greatly congested last night and this morning. There was seven or eight hours' delay by telegraph and two or three hours by telephone yesterday and both services are in an even worse plight today. The transmission of press messages has accordingly been a matter of unusual difficulty and I found it a much easier matter to communicate with London in the height of the Liverpool troubles last year than I did last night. The situation in Norwich with no electric light, no tramway or railway service, thousands of people unemployed and the normal life of the city disorganized, was yesterday and the day before very similar to that in Liverpool last August when the railway strike came on top of the riots, though the causes were vastly different.

The flood level stone in New Mills Yard charts the past inundations of the city of Norwich with the 1912 level chalked in above them all.

Shortly before the dinner hour some tram services were restored and by evening *The Times* correspondent was able to report, in a second despatch, that the sun had shone all afternoon and the worst of the floods were clearly over, the river was five feet below the maximum height of the previous day and was continuing to fall rapidly. The GER was gradually restoring its train , several London train were run and the Cromer service was restored in the afternoon flowed by the Mundesley branch and the line to the South of Beccles and Wymondham was reported as being free from floods. The citizens of Norwich who had been made homeless were, however, advised not to return to their dwelling by the Medical Officer of Health as he feared danger from the unhealthy conditions in which the floods have left the buildings.

During the night of Thursday 29 August the flood water began to rapidly drain away but took more buildings down with it and further houses were lost due to subsidence. Among these losses was The Ostrich, a Morgan's pub, kept by Albert Mace, that stood next to Kett's Castle at 31-33 Kett's Hill. Situated on a hill, the flood waters had not come near the place, at least above ground; below ground was a different story. The road on

Kett's Hill and the Ostrich had shown some evidence of subsidence on Wednesday morning and supports were placed against the building, but it was not thought serious enough to close the house which kept open until 10.30pm when the grave condition of the building had become so obvious the landlord got his wife and five children out of the house and he had almost removed all furniture and effects from within to other houses and premises on Kett's Hill when the entire frontage of the pub collapsed at 11.00pm. The bar, smoke room, and bottle and jug entrance on the ground floor were all wrecked along with, the sitting room and a bedroom on the first floor, four bedrooms on the second floor. An adjoining cottage occupied by a boot repairer named Pond was also torn town with the collapse. Despite a number of people being around at the time of the collapse, fortunately no-one was injured.[1]

The Ostrich public house on Kett's Hill after its collapse - another victim of subsidence caused by unprecedented underground water levels.

FRIDAY 30 AUGUST

By Friday morning the streets were practically free from water, the greatest depth in any public thoroughfare then being only two or three inches, rounds of food deliveries could be made and corporation electricity was gradually restored for power and lighting, much to relief of manufacturers and employees. Practically the whole plant had been under two feet of water at the height of the flood and much labour had been required to clear away the accumulation of mud on the machinery.

1 Author's Note: The Ostrich was rebuilt but closed in July 1939 and lay derelict for many years. When the building was finally demolished an old matchbox was discovered containing a message 'the front of this house fell down during the flood of August 1912 caused by the road falling in.'

AFTERMATH

The queue for flood relief at
St Andrew's Hall, Norwich

The Medical Officer of Health was charged with the medical arrangements for dealing with the people in the school refuges and a Clothing Committee, under Mrs. James Stuart, rendered useful service at the Technical Institute. Norwich citizens responded nobly to the appeal for clothing, bringing thousands of garments, underclothes, boots and shoes to the Technical School where they were dealt with by voluntary staff and lady helpers and a vast team behind the scenes who helped to sort out and mend the clothes as they arrived. So many clothes were donated the committee sent its surplus to rural areas of the county that had also been affected by the floods.

Initially flood relief had been handed out from the court room at the Guildhall, which took on the appearance of a harvest festival with its wooden forms occupied by row after row of corned beef and other food parcels donated by Norwich citizens while the corners were stacked with loaves of bread. Mr. E. J. W. Huggins, The indefatigable Clerk to the Guardians worked with his team of willing helpers to transform St Andrew's Hall into a food depot where food relief was served out to hundreds of applicants at St Andrew's Hall between Thursday 29 August and Thursday 5 September. Over a thousand loaves of bread were distributed along with vast quantities of corned beef and cheese. Long queues of people were to be seen between the hours of eleven and five. Most of those who came for relief were able to return to their homes but were unable to afford food owing to being temporarily unemployed as a number of the factories in the flooded district had been closed.

One utility that was maintained throughout the flooding was the supply of gas, thanks to the friendly assistance of a fire engine, afterwards supplanted by a portable engine, which was in turn flooded out and finally by a steam roller loaned by the civic authorities that enabled the gas company to keep their elevating and conveyer plant and pumps at work.

Despite having a significant part of their works swept away the *Norwich Mercury* did not miss an issue thanks to Messrs. Fletcher and Sons Ltd who kindly put their machinery and premises at the disposal of the newspaper.

Magnificent service was rendered at the various relief centres by Corporation officials and workmen, Guardians and Relieving Officers, Education Officials, School Attendance Officers, a large number of teachers along with the Territorials of the 2nd East Anglian Field Ambulance RAMC, indeed it was recorded 'without distinction of position or social standing, men and women of high and low degree responded to that one touch of nature which makes the whole kin.'

Having observed the scenes of devastation around Wymondham, John Burns, President of the Local Government Board paid a flying visit to the city to make a personal inspection of the flooded area. After travelling along many of the affected streets he met with the Acting Lord Mayor, the Chairman of the Board of the Guardians and the Town Clerk and expressed his pleasure at the organisation of the relief effort.

With the dissipation of the flood waters Norwich citizens began the massive task of clearing debris and cleaning up. The municipal departments and public services of the city had deployed their personnel effectively. Men had been posted on each of the bridges over the Wensum around the city to intercept the floating timber that had been carried away by the waters from the flooded wood yards by the river although they were unable to salvage many of the thousands of wood paving blocks that had been lifted from the streets and carried away by the waters.

A number of churches had their vaults inundated such as the historic St Clement's church where two feet of water was registered; fortunately someone had the presence of mind to rescue the parish registers that date back to 1538 from their fireproof safe in good time as it was later found to have filled with water.

Once the waters had receded many domestic and commercial items that had been lifted or carried away by the flood were left stranded in odd positions. In one house on Lothian Street, for instance, the swirl of the waters had swept furniture all over the place leaving the sewing machine on the floor clogged with mud and sand and the chairs and table upturned in a corner. A few doors on a piano was spread out to dry, laying on its back upon four chairs with water dripping out of its works.

There were rumours of an outbreak of pestilence in Norwich but there were unfounded. Dr E. P. Manby, one of the Medical Inspectors of the Local Government Board conferred with Mr G. Hervey, Local Government Poor Law Inspector, regarding the effects of the floods. Dr Manby had found little sewage had washed into the houses because the flood water was practically clean and it had fallen almost as quickly as it rose, thus there were only small amounts of smell or matter in most houses, the drinking water, although in short supply for a time, also remained uncontaminated. The Medical Officer of Health's return of infectious diseases for the 'Flood Week' showed only three cases of scarlet fever and three of diphtheria notified as occurring within the flooded area. One further case of diphtheria was removed from one of the shelters on Monday 26 August.

On the evening of Friday 13 September a meeting was held under the chairmanship of the Ven. Archdeacon Pelham in the Thatched Assembly Rooms, Norwich to firstly thank the Lord Mayor, the Corporation and the Board of Guardians for their prompt measures to relieve the distress of those affected by the floods and secondly, to urge the Corporation to deal with the whole matter of re-housing people from the flood damaged areas and other crowded parts of the city. A resolution to that effect was made, carried unanimously and duly forwarded to the Lord Mayor. The meeting was closed in a most impressive manner and those who were privileged to be present on that occasion would long remember the touching words uttered by the good archdeacon.

Norwich had been miraculously saved from serious loss of life during the floods but loss of life there had been, most prominent of all had been the death of George Brodie, the rescue worker who had died saving women and children. Considerable public sympathy had gathered and was exemplified by the large number of people who attended his funeral at Norwich Cemetery. The mourners were led by his wife and elderly mother, included among the wreaths was a handsome floral tribute from the Lord Mayor and Lady Mayoress of Norwich, accompanied by a card stating it was sent 'as a mark of deep sympathy and as a tribute to of respect to a true hero, who gave his life in a noble endeavour to save the lives of others.'

Close up of the people in the flood relief queue outside St Andrew's Hall. Many of those affected by the floods in Norwich were those who had little in the first place.

Flooded road at Church End, Walpole St Peter.

ACROSS THE COUNTY

THE RAINFALL OF 25-26 AUGUST 1912, RECORDED AT NORFOLK STATIONS AND COLLATED BY
ARTHUR W. PRESTON, F.R.MET.SOC., SECRETARY OF NORFOLK RAINFALL ORGANIZATION

Location	Inches		
Denver	3.92	Brundall	8.09
Wareham	4.24	Moulton	7.13
Sporle	2.72	North Repps	5.46
Dunham	3.57	Gunton	6.89
Watton	3.80	Worstead	5.89
Caston	3.85	Dilham	3.86
Gt. Witchingham	3.37	Hevingham (Rippon Hall)	6.05
Hingham	3.99	Acle	4.05
Wymondham	6.52	Ormesby	6.59
Hethersett	7.33	Great Yarmouth	5.12
Keswick	6.88	Dunston	7.22
Drayton	6.60	Swainsthorpe	7.01
Norwich (Eaton)	7.34	Saxlingham	6.65
Norwich (Ipswich Road)	7.36	Hedenham	4.03
Norwich (Cemetery)	7.51	Geldeston	4.43

The readings were for a 48 hour period ending at 9am on 27 August, entered according to their usual rule as for 25 and 26; as the rain did not commence until 3.00 or 4.00am on 26 August, the total amounts recorded fell in a period of 29-30 hours.

ACLE

All railway traffic was stopped about midday on Monday 26 August. About fifty feet of the railway embankment, the Yarmouth side of Acle station and on the north side of the line gave way through the heavy rain and began slowly sliding down towards the signalman's house and garden, until the heavy palings gave way with the great weight, and tons of it came down only just short of the rails. On the south side there were two large crevices where tons of the embankment gave way and fell into a garden, covering all the vegetables. The county road, for about 100 yards each side of the railway bridge and under it was impassable and in some places the water was over two feet deep. The road towards the Run Bridge was under water as well as the Yarmouth New Road by the four cross-ways.

ATTLEBOROUGH

Attleborough stands on high ground but all the roads leading to it were submerged and almost impassable on Monday night. The turnpike from Norwich was flooded in two places and motor cars in several cases were either held up for the night or had to turn round to seek a new route. A number of passengers on the GER who had been held up at Wymondham and accommodation finding the accommodation there limited there were sent on to Attleborough. All hotels were thus filled in the town and several private houses took in stranded people.

The first place to flood in Attleborough was always at the junction of Station and New North Roads and true to form this point was submerged by noon on Monday. Most people took advantage of the wall that ran along the station allotments. The most striking sight was the flooded stream that cuts across the north of Attleborough. This was normally two yards across but the drainage from the fields increased it to a full hundred yards in width. Bannister Bridge was entirely surrounded by a 'broad' and on Tuesday a local carter took advantage of the unusual conditions by ferrying pedestrians across at a 'penny return.'

AYLSHAM AND DISTRICT

Considerable damage was caused at Aylsham when the river overflowed its banks at Millgate and flooded the area. The M&GN station was rendered unapproachable except by wading waist deep through water and cottagers took to their bedrooms. On the evening of Monday 26 August the Yarmouth train was held up at the station. There were upwards of 200 passengers and with the exception who got through the water into the town they had to spend the night in the train. Late at night Mr. T. W. Purdy, with Mr F. C. Buckingham and other helpers managed to get milk to the children on board the train and provisions were afterwards got to the other passengers. Pigs and chickens were floating about in the water, many of them were drowned, the passengers on the train being much disturbed by the squealing as they died. Trees fell to the ground in a number of places including the orchard of Mr Butterfield on Burgh Road and the bridge at **Ingworth** was swept away severing the road connecting Aylsham and Cromer.

The public road to the Midland and Great Northern Railway Station, Millgate, Aylsham 27 August 1912.

The *Norwich Mercury* reporter attempting to visit Aylsham on Tuesday morning found the journey would have been impossible for vehicular traffic. At **Marsham** the road was flooded to a considerable depth and the reporter only managed to get through by shouldering his bicycle and walking along the top of a fence. At **Hevingham** he found the road bridge had been washed away and only managed to get across by means of a ladder. Between **Stratton Strawless** and St Faith's the telegraph wires were strewn across the road and on arrival at **St Faith's** he found the bridge partially collapsed but there was still space left for passage.

Floods at Millgate, Aylsham with some of the houses on Mash's Row in the background 27 August 1912

BESTHORPE

This village suffered badly from flooding. Cottagers at Silver Street were driven to take refuge in the upper rooms and stock keepers had great difficulty in saving cattle and pigs, but in most cases the animals sought their own salvation. A bull calf that had fallen in a ditch brought help and rescue by his continual bellowing. The only casualties suffered were a large quantity of drowned chickens.

BLAKENEY AND CLEY

The fresh water cutting and drain near Blakeney were much swollen by 9.00am on Monday 26 August. Valuable stock grazing on the meadows were secure and transferred to stables in pitiless rain. As the day wore on whenever a sign of abatement appeared evident it was immediately followed by the increased violence of the storm and a heavy wind from the north made many of the roads almost impassable. On the low-lying meadows and fields there were considerable quantities of corn cut and when the creeks overflowed the corn was washed away.

The small waterway on the Cley Road from Holt, known locally as 'The Watering' soon assumed the dimensions of a river and the Glaven, particularly at Glandford made the usual ford impassable. The road from Cley to Blakeney was covered to a depth of over two feet and made communication impossible and many houses suffered flooding to a depth of about two feet of water inside them, while the meadow used for circuses and fairs stood several feet deep. To the east the same conditions prevailed, the enormous stretch of marshes resembled a huge broad and cut the coast road off.

CAISTER

Water found its way into a number of cottages at Caister flooding the lower rooms to a considerable depth. Vanda Villas were badly flooded and the Caister Golf Ground was under water.

At the Socialist Holiday camp the hundred campers there experienced a lively time. The tents were storm swept, many being blown down and badly damaged and Mr. and Mrs. Fletcher Dodd spared no pains to provide accommodation elsewhere for their campers. Fortunately there were a number of commodious recreation rooms and other places where the ladies and gentlemen were soon comfortably ensconced.

All that was left of Costessey Bridge after the flood.

COSTESSEY

All approaches to Costessey were cut off, excepting through Costessy Park by the lodge gate entrance on Dereham Road. The bridge between Costessey and Taverham was submerged. The bridge in Earlham Field Lane was swept away, the footbridge in Water Lane was buckled and the ford impassable.

The intense rainfall of August 1912 caused this cliff fall at Cromer.

CROMER AND DISTRICT

A man was driving down the road in the direction of Cromer and had just passed over one bridge when it collapsed as his wheels regained the roadway. Half a mile further down the road another bridge he had to pass over broke down just before he got to it and thus he found himself marooned between two impassable bridges.

A newspaper correspondent at Cromer wrote on Wednesday 28 August:

We were entirely cut off from the outer world from about midday on Monday until this morning, when a few letters and papers got through. Never have I seen anything distantly approaching the scenes of Monday. From our dining room window we saw umbrellas one after another torn to shreds; people clutching railings at corners to hold themselves up and some of the pedestrians actually blown to the ground. And the rain! I determined to have a look at the sea and I was barely across the road before water was streaming off my mackintosh down my legs.

Yesterday morning, before and after breakfast everyone here went to look at the devastating effects of the storm. Thousands of tons of cliff must have fallen. In fully a half dozen places the parade was practically impassable owing to the debris; deep gullies were cut in the roads by torrents of water; some of the public lamp posts had their heads bent over till they almost resembled a shepherd's crook. Most of the bathing tents were either buried or torn to fragments; even some of the solid huts were overthrown of shifted from their moorings.

The cliffs at Cromer and along the coast suffered badly in the storm, the Coastguard cliff at Cromer was undermined, at Runton the septic tanks were damaged and many boats buried by cliff fall. At Sidestrand the old parish church tower, the centre of Clement Scott's *Garden of Sleep*, had been left very near the edge of the cliff after yet another cliff fall.

COLTISHALL, HAUTBOIS AND HORSTEAD

Collapsed cottages at Coltishall

Dr E. P. Manby, one of the Medical Inspectors of the Local Government Board conferred with the County Medical Officer for Health, Dr. Nash regarding the flooding in the rural districts around Norwich as they drove around the county in early September. As far as they could ascertain, although many families had been made homeless by the floods, little permanent damage to dwellings had occurred, with the exception of eight cottages that had collapsed in Coltishall and Great Hautbois where a number of houses collapsed and five or six more adjoining The White Horse Hotel had been seriously damaged and would probably have to be demolished. These houses were constructed of clay lump, as were many old cottages in Norfolk and the floods simply dissolved the lower part of their walls. Coltishall Bridge, however, had suffered severe damage; a huge gap had been torn through it by the flood waters and crossing was only possible by boat.

The huge gap torn in Coltishall Bridge by the flood engorged waters of the River Bure.

The Recruiting Sergeant public house and Norwich Road under flood at Horstead.

Hay stacks were swept away from the meadows of Lammas and Hautbois damming the river by the narrow Coltishall bridge. When this gave way the water levels suddenly dropped, exposing the bed of the dam by Buxton Mill.

The view across where the bridge had stood to the subsided road and The Anchor of Hope, Lammas

View from Anchor of Hope towards the shattered remnant of the bridge and the boat that provided a ferry crossing in the absence of the bridge.

The temporary bridge that restored a connection between between Buxton and Lammas while a new bridge was built on the site of the one that had been destroyed by the flood waters.

DEREHAM

The town escaped the main horrors of Monday's deluge and inundations but it did not escape unscathed. The most distressing sight in the town was in Bath Avenue where many gardens were covered in water, some of the basements were flooded with dirty water to a depth of three of four feet and tenants forced to retreat to upper rooms and livestock such as ducks and rabbits were only rescued in the nick of time. These floods were one of the results of the enormous accumulation of water on the Neatherd Moor. Beyond the gardens it was literally a river that pursued its way through Mr. Gray's stackyard to Norwich Road. Here the drains were unable to cope with the volume of water and the road became flooded for a distance of about 150 yards and to a depth of over two feet in places. A number of the council roadman were set to work to get rid of as much of the water as possible but were only able to do so by cutting courses through the bank into a field. Nearly all Tuesday, however, it was necessary to use one of the council's carts to convey pedestrians over the flooded portion. A number of trees were also blown down in the same neighbourhood, a number were also made unstable by the gale and a telephone wire was broken.

At Washbridge a very large area was completely submerged; several houses narrowly escaped being flooded and access was only possible at the back. Some of the residents experienced much anxiety with their live stock and in one case men were busy until the early hours of Tuesday morning removing pigs and other animals to safety. Large portions of the roads as well as gardens at South Green and Toftwood were under water of some feet and a council cart was also provided here to convey pedestrians through the flood. Motor vehicles also found the going difficult here and a car and a coal wagon were temporarily stranded.

Above left: The floods on Norwich Road, East Dereham (*Kitty Lynn*)

Above right: Shipdam Road, Toftwood, near East Dereham (*Kitty Lynn*)

Right: Washbridge, East Dereham (*Kitty Lynn*)

DOWNHAM MARKET

The abnormal height of the water in St John's Eau meant the lower parts of the town were unable to get rid of the tremendous quantity of water which rushed down from the higher parts and as a consequence a number of fields and gardens quickly became flooded and several highways in the vicinity were rendered impassable for pedestrians. Water also reached within a few inches of the furnaces of the Downham Gas and Coke Company and but for the prompt and assiduous work of Mr. H. Castleton and staff the gas supply of the town might easily have been spoilt. At **Fincham** the water was from two to three feet deep in places and several cottagers had to be removed from their dwellings in tumbrils.

FAKENHAM

A record rainfall of about six inches fell at Fakenham. Nothing approaching the flooding experienced there had been known in the town since 1878 when the overflow of the river was equally alarming. The filed around the town were inundated presenting one vast sea of water dotted with occasional islets here and there, punctuated by upstanding trees and human habitations cut off from their neighbours by water.

River overflowing its banks near Fakenham Mill on 27 August 1912

The Causeway leading to Fakenham Town Station was described as a 'miniature Niagra' and the roadway a rushing torrent, on the outskirts of which several hundred onlookers congregated and a rich harvest of coppers was reaped by owners of vehicles who were busily employed in conveying pedestrians around the town. Fears were constantly expressed that the causeway might give way under the stress of water so a waterway was cut through to avoid such a calamity. Mill Lane and Hall Staithe suffered considerably and many of the houses were flooded and the unfortunate occupants had to seek refuge upstairs.

Mr. Gogg's mill was also partly under water and a huge tree close by was uprooted and fell athwart the stream. Three unfortunate cows had a narrow escape from drowning on Tuesday evening. Having rushed on the Recreation Ground adjoining the river they were carried by the flood waters to the other side of the river where they were found the following morning, huddled together on a small piece of high ground, to the great relief of their owner.

Above left: The level of the river has almost risen to the height of the flood waters around Fakenham Mill, 27 August 1912

Above right: The rescue and food supply party during the floods at Walsingham.

The Gas Works were isolated, but fortunately escaped inundation and the continual working of the pumps kept the furnaces free from water. The new sewerage operations were, however, seriously hindered and some anxiety was caused by the great influx of water into the trenches and the cellar of the house adjoining occupied by Mr R. Tuck, a baker.

DISS AND DISTRICT

The official record, kept by the Medical Officer of Health for Diss, showed that between 2.00am and 11pm on Monday the rainfall was 5.43 inches, and between 2.00am and 9.00am on Monday morning one and a half inches were recorded. Diss was fortunate in that it did not suffer major damage. The floods that did affect the town ran from Church Street to Sandy Lane, running parallel with the main thoroughfare through the town. Sandy Lane was flooded but the houses escaped with comparatively little damage. Messrs. Chaplyn's Malting in Victoria Road and cottages nearby were also flooded.

The precautions taken by the Surveyor on Monday morning saved the flooding of the houses in Church Street. Mr Cooper ordered a hole to be cut through a bank and personally superintended the work. Lower down, however, some cottages behind the Gas Works were surrounded with water and the basements flooded. So serious was the position Messrs. Hasted, Nurse, R. Youngs and Beckett used the skiff, that belonged to Mr Beckett, to get to work on Tuesday morning. More serious for the town as a whole was the flooding of the Gas Works.

On Monday night there was water to the depth of two feet five inches in the cellars under the regenerators. The manager of the works, Mr. Gibbs, set a gang of men at work pumping, but they could only get the water down to sixteen inches though they laboured until 6.00am. The fires were rendered useless and after 3.00pm no gas was made. The manager ordered the old 'direct fire' plant, which was superseded five years ago, to be brought into use, and after some hours delay the fire were 'picked up' and the holders began to rise. No gas was made for forty-eight hours, there was a restricted supply on Wednesday but in the middle of the day the old plant began to fill the holders, which by that time were nearly empty.

Beyond the railway arch the over-flow of the Waveney had caused a great flood and Scole was completely cut off from Diss. In the main street of this village on Monday at noon there was two feet of water and the Harleston roadway was a torrent. Several cars stopped in the main street and had to be dragged out by horses. From Tuesday, post men with rural rounds were provided with carts to carry out the rounds but still found some of their routes impassable.

Hundreds of acres adjacent to the River Waveney and its tributaries were under water. The damage done is enormous, not only to crops but to cottages, and in many small villages the damage was estimated at several hundred pounds.

There was much water on the road from Diss to Scole, the low-lying land on either side being covered, but the flood was even deeper on the main road to Ipswich near Scole Bridge and parts of Scole suffered inundations. The youngsters in the parish, however, treated the disaster light heartedly and Mr Roy Wilson was seen swimming in the lane outside his father's house.

The neighbouring parish and Billingford suffered severely and a number of cottagers were driven to taken refuge in their upstairs rooms. At Shimpling the flood seemed worse than anywhere else in the district. From Langmere, the other side of Dickleburgh to Shimpling, the roadway was flooded with water that rushed down to the hill with the force of a torrential stream and did much devastation. Pigs, turkeys and chickens were drowned in scores and more cottagers were driven upstairs and were isolated. One labourer said the inhabitants of his bedroom consisted of himself, his wife and three children, ten ferrets, a pig and a dog. The flood seems to have swept through Burston and Frenze into the river. Dickleburgh Street was partly under water but little damage was done. Oakley also suffered in the floods, fences and hedges were swept down and a bridge on the road from Oakley to Billingford was so damaged as to be impassable.

EAST TUDDENHAM

Two or three hundred yards along the main turnpike road to Norwich a huge cave was washed in side of the road, extending dangerously near the line of traffic. The opening was about a yard deep and 4ft across.

FLEGG DISTRICT

Havoc was wrought by the floods throughout the Flegg district. At Rollesby Workhouse the rain drove through the roofs of one of the wards and it was found necessary to remove the inmates to another part of the house and a chimney was blown down. In the workhouse garden, the damage was very great. A number of fruit tress were uprooted and a summer house that had been a favourite among the older inmates was completely wrecked. The cellars under the Workhouse were flooded to a depth of several inches. In Mr. Pigden's garden, thirty-six fruit trees were destroyed by the storm and the whole of the large fruit crops ruined. Mr. Allard and other fruit growers sustained similar losses.

So great was the volume of water that the twin ponds at **Martham** were speedily filled and formed a huge lake. The water found its way into the back premises of several of those residing nearby. In the meantime another torrent poured down White Street and flooded three cottages occupied by Messrs, Guymer, Hobbs and Bell. The occupants were forced to take refuge in their upper rooms. The storm was terribly destructive, many large trees being uprooted and thrown across the roads, completely blocking them. Great anxiety prevailed respecting the safety of livestock on the marshes which had been submerged and several cattle fell into dykes. The men worked hard to get the cattle home and in most cases they were successful but Mr. F. Gooch and Mr. Myhill lost a number of valuable bullocks which were found on Tuesday drowned in the deep dykes.

The 'new river' that appeared on Repps Road, Martham, 26 August 1912.

Flood water and one of the downed trees at Martham, 27 August 1912.

Mr. Francis, jnr. had a narrow escape during the storm. He went to fetch his child from school and while retuning along Church Road, found that he had to wade through water up to his waist in order to reach home. At one point he halted to consider what was the best road to take and just then a large elm tree was blown down just ahead of him, But for his momentary hesitation both himself and child would probably have been killed.

A large pond at Ormesby overflowed onto the roadway and speedily caused a flood several feet deep. The water swept into Col. Edis's pool opposite the Old Hall and this overflowing found its way into the gardens and a number of cottages lying in a valley near the church. All the lower rooms were flooded and the inhabitants were driven upstairs. The worst disaster occurred to three cottages occupied by Messrs Woolston, Knights and Smith. The gardens were submerged to a depth of over six feet and the cottages were rapidly flooded up to the top of the lower room windows and the cottagers left unable to remove any of the contents. Mr Palmer lost the whole of his valuable winter crops of apples and pears, together with most of the trees. Among the other losses, Mr G. Nichols had the gable end of a barn blown out and the roof partly destroyed.

At Ormesby St Michael nearly all the houses were rendered almost uninhabitable by reason of the rain forcing its way under the roofs. A considerable acreage of oats was lying in a veritable lake of water and rendered almost worthless.

FORNCETT ST PETER, BUNWELL AND ASLACTON AND HAPTON

All of these villages were three or four feet deep in water and flood waters at a depth of six feet were recorded by the Safety Valve Inn. Corn was seen floating over the field while at the station the stranded passengers spent the night in waiting rooms and signal boxes. At **Tharston**, Messrs.Pearse and Sons water mills suffered badly and some furniture was swept away.

GISSING

A wedding had been arranged and the rector valiantly waded through the flood waters to the church only to find the party had not turned up – but then the water in the village had risen to a depth of four feet in places.

HARLESTON

A rain fall of some 3.94 inches in the space of a day was recorded at Harleston on Monday. The Post Office was made unapproachable except by wading through yards of water and cottagers had to be rescued from upstairs windows. Harleston was cut off from the surrounding country- to the sound, by an immense flood in the Waveney Valley and towards Scole by a landslip at Needham that blocked the entire highway to vehicular traffic. Large holes were washed in the road and at **Starston** and Harleston the swollen Beck swept away the railing and swept away fences. The mail carts that came from Bungay on Monday night only reached the town by a circuitous route, via Aldeburgh, through fields and dangerous floods. The railway at **Homersfield** was flooded to such an extent to stop traffic and severe damage was suffered by Homersfield Station. Part of the platform had collapsed and the wooden railway bridge and bank were washed away leaving just metals and sleepers suspended in the air. The County Council bridge situated close by, was undermined and settled to an alarming extent. During Tuesday the bridge and the road between Mendham Street and the River Waveney collapsed and the iron bridge over the river had one side listed by the pressure of the water and overturned.

The aftermath of the flooding around Homersfield Station.

HEMPSTEAD

Waters overflowed at Hempstead Water Mill and at Selbrigge Pond. The pressure became so great that a large portion of the wall next to the road surrounding the garden was suddenly carried away, the water surging through in immense volume carrying all before it and tearing up the road on its course. The mill and house adjoining were surrounded and inundated by water.

The full effect of this tremendous burst of water was felt for miles along the course of the river which passed through Edgefield, Hunworth, Stody, Thornage and Letheringsett. At the bottom of the steep hill leading from Holt to Edgefield, the bridge over the road was carried away by the waters, leaving a chasm of fifteen feet wide and ten feet deep.

Below left: Hempstead Mill, August 1912.

Below right: Subsidence caused by the flooding on the road at Hempstead.

HEMSBY

A number of cottages in the low lying parts of the village were flooded out and all their lower rooms rendered uninhabitable.

HETHERSETT AND GREAT MELTON

The road from Hethersett to Great Melton was submerged to such an extent that after three attempts the postman had to relinquish the afternoon delivery of letters there and after sending the evening despatch of letter to the station through water nearly up to the bottom of the cart, only to find the trains not running. The Postmaster had to send the mail bags to Norwich by road. Workshops had to be surrendered to the invading flood and farmers who had stock in low meadows had to remove them under much difficulty to a place of safety and in some of the cow houses the water was a high as the mangers.

HOLME

Whitehall Farm House was inundated with water, which gained an entrance through the stopping of a surface water drain. The ground floor of the residence was flooded and all the surrounding gardens converted into a lagoon, while the tenant, his family and visitors were driven to take refuge in the upper floors.

HUNWORTH

The bridge over the road from Edgefield broke up under the force of the flood waters. At the Old Hunworth Mill House the usual water course was totally inadequate to carry off the water and for a long time this mill and the mill house acted as a dam holding up the waters that rose in the adjoining roads and meadows, to such an extent that it afterwards swept round, destroying the upper pond (one of five sources of water that fed the mill at the time) and swirled around the mill and house with great force, tearing away the roadway to the Mill House and placing the occupants in danger, swamping the house with water to a height of three feet inside.

Many rescuers came to help in the risky efforts to get the occupier, his wife and seven children out and a baker's cart laden with bread got stuck in the river and had to be abandoned until the following day. At this spot between Hunworth and Thornage acres of ground were under water.

HONINGHAM

Two bridges were broken down by the torrential waters. Honingham Hall was surrounded by about eighteen inches of water but by the efforts of the state men under the direction of Sir Ailwyn Fellowes and his estate agent the water was kept out of the hall. The lake and river banks broke away and caused a great breadth of water but the picturesque bridge at the entrance drive was washed away. Bits of foot bridges, coops and fowl houses, fencing, gates, vegetables and bee hives were all seen floating in the waters. The mill and mill house stood in great danger until the bridge gave way.

The marshland around King's Lynn also suffered from the deluge. The dykes and drains filled to overflowing and as the pumping stations were unable to cope with the flood waters, vast areas became submerged. On higher ground the land assumed the appearance of large inland lagoons and whole districts were flooded to the extent some areas were under four to six feet of water.

Banks and dams gave way under the strain and scores of countryside cottages were flooded out. In the valleys of the Ouse and Nar the water flowed over instead of under the bridges, several of which were carried away. Hundreds of heads of poultry, pigs and sheep were drowned during Monday night and there were many exciting rescues of stock, men wading over the flooded pastures to drive cattle onto safer ground.

Early on Tuesday morning a breakdown gang left Lynn to deal with a goods train which had fallen through a collapsed culvert on the GER between Fakenham and Walsingham. Just as the engine passed over the structure the culvert gave way, making a gap sixty feet long and several of the trucks were derailed.

LETHERINGSETT

The whole of the lower portion of The Street and along the course of the Glaven was one mass of water. Boats had to be used in the street to gain access to many houses.

LODDON

On Monday 26 August The Beck overflowed its banks and the flood waters spread over several acres. At 11pm the water rose with alarming rapidity and at midnight a portion of the road near the bridge gave way and part of the bridge collapsed. The Mill, owned by Messrs. Wood, Sadd, Moore and Co. was in great danger and a gang of forty men worked all night to successfully preserve it. The pilings and banks of the Chet were washed away and sherries broke from their moorings. The GER motor bus was on the Norwich Road but nearing Framingham the water reached the engine and the bus was obliged to remain on the road all night.

Above left: Temporary bridge and embankment near the mill at Loddon 28 August 1912.

Above right: The damage left by the floods at the mill at Loddon, 28 August 1912.

LONG STRATTON

Swan Lane was submerged and householders in the adjoining streets took refuge in their bedrooms. When the water subsided practically all the cottages were left unsafe and the roads were left 'in a deplorable condition.'

LUDHAM

At Ludham, a number of trees were uprooted by the gale, several falling across the roads. The telegraph wire was broken by a falling tree on the Yarmouth Road. Two roads were so flooded as to be impassable on foot. Tiles were blown off houses, the penetrating rain in some instances kept inhabitants continuously employed in baling out water.

MARKSHALL

At noon on Tuesday the cart of Mr Pimm, a Norwich grocer, was about to cross the small bridge immediately over the river bridge at Markshall, which was deeply flooded. Part of the bridge had been washed away, although it could not be seen and the horse walked into the hole on the bridge. The driver and his companion were quickly out of the cart and did their best to save the horse but it was unfortunately drowned and the cart left to remain in the stream on the bridge.

MATTISHALL

The rain flooded several of the roads in Mattishall, especially the turnpike road to Norwich. People walking back from an auction had the unpleasant experience of wading through a long stretch of water which came up over their knees. Several persons hailed with joy a miller's wagon which came along just in time to pick up reluctant bathers. Cornfields were lying under water and some cottages were inundated. Men were seen to be busy on Tuesday morning clearing sheaves of corn out of the river with a crowd of spectators looking on at this unusual sight.

MULBARTON

The roads in and around Mulbarton were flooded to the depth of three feet in places. Six houses known as Mulbarton Factory were flooded. The inmates were driven into their bedrooms with the exception of Mr. and Mrs. Stebbings with their seven children, who had to abandon their home entirely and were given shelter in the Wingfield Hall for the night.

MUNDESLEY

The low-lying districts were inundated and parts of the grassy slopes at the promenade were washed away.

NEWTON FLOTMAN

The mill bridge covering the main road over the river had collapsed, only cyclists, foot passengers and very light vehicles being allowed over. One house in the back street almost collapsed, the end being washed away: fortunately the occupants had already evacuated having been washed out. At the Maid's Head the cellar filled with four feet of water and barrels of beer and cases floated out of the house and were carried to the river and men

Workmen set about clearing up after the destruction of the bridge between Forncett Junction and Flordon.

The waters of the North Walsham and Dilham Canal overflowed near Royston Bridge.

had to wade through the water waist deep to move their women and children to safety. The viaduct over the river between **Flordon and Forncett** Junction collapsed and the main road from Flordon to Tasburgh was also blocked by fallen trees and high water.

On Monday night the sub-postmaster at **Stratton Strawless** was driving to **Newton St Faith's** with letters. He was crossing the stream at **Haynford** when the horse and trap were caught by the force of the stream and carried down. The postmaster was swept against a fence which enabled him to get into safety, but the horse was drowned. The sub-postmaster at Newton St Faith's went out to meet him and was stopped on the road back by two large trees which had fallen across the road, taking with them the whole of the telegraph wires. Before he could proceed on his homeward journey he had to procure assistance and a saw to cut a way through the fallen timber.

NORTH WALSHAM

The GER Station had about 30ft of its brick wall of the subway washed away by the torrents of water from the permanent way and tons of earth was carried with it down the slope into the road. Under the two railway bridges near the stations where there were about 6ft of water, rendering the road impassable.

The bridge that spanned a stream over the road from Swafield to Bradfield collapsed leaving a gaping chasm, cutting off traffic. The North Walsham and Dilham Canal overflowed at Royston Bridge leaving the road nearby under about 1ft of water and the river at Ebridge Mills carried part of the bridge away and the flood waters ripped up the roadway, laying drain pipes bare and flooding Messrs. Cubitt & Walker's granary at the mill causing several hundred pounds worth of damage to the corn therein.

PULHAM ST MARY

Many houses were flooded in the village and residents were driven to their upstairs rooms by the inundation. Towards the evening food was conveyed to the stranded householders via their bedroom windows, reached by ladder. The cellar of the Maid's Head was flooded to the depth of six feet and the boarded fence about thirty feet long was washed away. Four miles along the Beck, a tributary of the River Waveney, the meadows, field, orchards and gardens were considerably flooded and garden produce was washed out of the ground and fowls, animals and various articles were carried away by the force of the water. The mid-day mail for Harleston did not leave, nor were there any afternoon letters from Harleston, the roads being absolutely impassable.

SAXLINGHAM

One of the few losses of human life outside the city occurred at Saxlingham. Holt postman, James Starling was near the blacksmith's shop where a covered culvert crosses the road where the water carried by it is hardly noticeable in normal circumstances. Starling had passed and repassed over the same road three times on Tuesday and on returning to Holt it seems he expected to get across although the water was surging across the road, over the culvert. A large hole had appeared in it and the rush of water being so great he was sucked in and carried through the culvert. His body was not found until the following morning when it was discovered in some meadows about three hundred yards away. Starling was aged over fifty years and a well respected man.

Harry Culley's delivery cart down the subsided culvert at Saxlingham.

Shortly after the tragic accident to the postman, a covered cart belonging to Mr H. Culley, a Holt grocer, was passing over the same spot when one of the wheels of the cart plunged down the hole and the men were only able to save themselves by climbing to the top of the cart cover. Help was soon on the scene, the men were removed to safely, the horse was extricated from the shafts and the cart left down the hole until the following day.

SCARNING

At the railway arch motor cars had to be drawn through the water by horses on Tuesday evening. Scarning Fen and Rushmeadow were submerged and a lot of water accumulated on Rushmeadow Road. Further along at the bridge the strong and furious river had struck a weak spot in the road and washed away a quantity of earth, leaving quite a hole. Some of the **Gressenhall** roads were deeply flooded and rendered almost impassable near the river.

SURLINGHAM

The waters rose to a very great height and the street was flooded near the Post Office. Some excitement was caused by a postman having a narrow escape in trying to cycle through but was carried to the bridge by the current. Two men on a horse tried to get through but the current overbalanced the horse, these men also fell into the water and were carried to the bridge and were lucky to make their escape. The marshes between Surlingham and Yarmouth were completely submerged.

SAXTHORPE AND CORPUSTY

The mill meadows were submerged and the stone bridge from the mill to Saxthorpe village was washed away as well as those at Little London and Corpusty.

A few planks provide a somewhat precarious temporary crossing where the Corpusty Mill bridge stood before the floods.

In country areas shooting rats became 'the sport' of the floods. Thousands of rodents took refuge in the high branches of trees and folks in boats and motor launches took to this golden opportunity to eradicate these vermin by shooting them. Rats clinging to the tops of gates were often dispatched with a swift blow from a sturdy stick. Hundreds of moles met a similar fate.

SHERINGHAM

The storm over the town during Monday increased in violence until it became a perfect blizzard of wind and rain. The rain appeared to come down in sheets of water, swamping and drenching everything and everywhere and penetrated roofs and walls, making houses wet and damp inside. At 9.30am the signal gun at the Coast Guard Station was fired to summon the lifeboat crew. Some of the fishing boats were in difficulty off Runton but managed to get to shore without assistance from the lifeboat. The lower part of Beeston Road was flooded with two of three feet of water. Chimney stacks suffered, tiles were torn off, windows were blown in and telegraph lines were brought down. The Arcade Lawn (Liedam's Entertainers) was demolished and the company adjourned to the Town Hall. Rain poured through the bell turret at St Peter's, making the west end of the church a kind of swamp. Many tents were destroyed and there was sad havoc in gardens and nurseries.

SPROWSTON

Mary Atkinson of Pearce's Field, Sprowston, had a narrow escape on Monday afternoon at about 3.00pm when she was walking by the side of a wall near her home when the ground suddenly gave way under her and finding herself being taken down under the wall by the falling earth, she shouted for help. Her cries were answered by Mr. Chapman and others who came to her rescue and fortunately managed to recover her in time. It was then found that a dead well existed in the corner of the hole, which was large enough to bury a horse and cart. About six or seven similar holes appeared in the vicinity.

SWAFFHAM

In 1912 British Army manoeuvres of an unprecedented scale in Great Britain were due to be conducted across East Anglia. They almost did not take place at all after torrential rain fall caused extensive flooding and drowned a number of camps that had been set up prior to commencement. The troops from 1st and 2nd Coldstream Guards and 2nd and 3rd Grenadier Guards arrived at Swaffham on Saturday 24 August. The weather experienced during the morning had made it impossible for the troops to occupy the meadows where their tents had been pitched and 1st Coldstreams were immediately sent back by train (to await an improvement in the weather), one battalion was left on the camp ground and the rest of the men, around 2,000 in number, had to be found billets. Police Superintendent George Flint stepped into the breach and helped to find accommodation for the soldiers in a variety of building through the town including the Assembly Room, Salvation Army Hall, the White Hart and King's Arms Inn, the Drill Hall, the Infant's and Boy's Schools, the Vicarage Room, the malting of Vynne & Everett, Messrs. F. And G. Preston's and Messrs. Chamberlain and Co's granaries and barns owned by Mr. W. Quadling and Mr. Smith.

Rain fell heavily during the night but on Sunday the weather conditions improved and the soldiery were engaged in shifting tents to another field and boarding the floors. Soldiers not engaged in field work attended the Sunday service at the parish church. A great number

Camp life at Swaffham.

The flooded Guards camp at Swaffham

Drummers of 2nd Battalion, The Grenadier Guards in their emergency billet at the Assembly Rooms, Swaffham.

Drums, 2nd Battalion Grenadier Guards Billeted in Assembly rooms.

of townsfolk and people from the surrounding villages visited throughout the day and the soldiers left their billets to occupy their tents for Sunday night. On Monday morning the storm clouds opened at 3.00am and the deluge began here. The camping ground soon became a quagmire and one of the fields to which one of the camps had been removed took on the appearance of a lake leaving some of the tents in two of three feet of water and the roadway became a river and the drenched soldiers were evacuated to their previous billets of Saturday night.

After weathering the worst days of the storm the soldiers set about the business of preparing for the manoeuvres, a correspondent from *The Times*, recorded: 'As I stand by the side of a Norfolk turnpike, this inimitable infantry swung by, wet to the skin, perhaps chilled to the marrow, chanting a roundelay to prove it takes more than weather to fathom the bottom of the *esprit* of British infantry.' On 12 September the correspondent's despatch recounted: 'Today, thank goodness, a change has come. The bitter north wind has dropped, the mists have rolled away off the Norfolk Broads and the kindly sun has dried the wringing khaki of the gallant men.' With the weather improved the manoeuvres went ahead as planned.

The swollen River Thet rises high under the bridge at Thetford.

THETFORD

The rainfall around the Thetford area and the ensuing flooding was not as severe as in other parts of the county. The fields here were flooded but the light, sandy soil that characterises the district helped to absorb a lot of the water. In Thetford the river rose considerably and overflowed into the adjacent fields opposite the Haling path and the rain, driven by a strong wind, penetrated beneath the slates and tiles of many houses. Mr Greenwood at the Water Works reported that during the twenty nine hours preceding 9.00am on Tuesday morning as much as 4.68 inches of rain was registered.

THORNAGE

The bridge over the main road was slightly damaged. In the street at Thornage the walls of the gardens and cottages belonging to Mr. Boardman of Norwich were knocked down by the force of the large body of water coming from the direction of Brinton. Nearby, in the meadows, a large marquee owned by Mr. Hole of The Mount, Edgefield, that was used for religious services was reduced to shreds leaving forms and chairs floating on the flood waters. At Brinton itself many houses were also flooded.

TIVETSHALL

A member of Norwich Mercury staff recorded his experiences after leaving a meeting of the Board of Guardians he set off for Norwich:

Leaving the workhouse just before noon the low road to Tivetshall Station was almost impassable and there were two or three stretches at least two hundred yards in

The floods around Thornage Bridge 26 August 1912

length where the road was quite submerged. In places the water was more than two feet deep and with the fields on either side flooded there was no alternative to the uninviting prospect of a wade through the swirling waters. The scene was a memorable one. The water was rushing on to the road in enormous volumes, tearing the surface of the highway from the foundations in its mad career. At the Gateways it ran off the fields like a mountain torrent and at intervals along the hedgerows, where the pressure of water was heaviest, it burst the fences and poured through a miniature waterfalls and helped to swell the surging river in the road. Standing barley was completely covered [with flood water] and elsewhere the corn 'cocked' in preparation for carting stood like sugar loaf islets in vast sheets of water. The rain drove across the country in dense clouds and no matter how well protected, nobody could venture forth for many minutes without being drenched to the skin.

WELLS AND DISTRICT

At **Wells** several trees were blown down while yachts and boats broke from their moorings. Mr. Robert Claxton of **Wighton** had an exceedingly narrow escape on Tuesday 27 August; when he was driving home near the bottom of Wighton Hill the bridge collapsed and his horse and cart fell into the river. Fortunately Mr. Claxton was able to grab a hold upon the wall and saved himself but sadly the horse was drowned. Communication with other villages in the area failed on Monday and was only restored to the western parts of the settlements on Wednesday when the waters abated there. The waters at the horsepit at **Morston** rapidly overflowed and formed a watery barrier by the church wall. The scene at **Stiffkey**, was more serious, cottages and stables were flooded in the main street and a number of people were evacuated to Warborough House. At the White Bridges it was estimated the flood water was eight feet deep and at the height of the flood a boy from Blakeney drove or rather swam his master's horse and cart through a 'seething maelstrom' of flood waters near the White Bridges against the warnings of the locals and was considered lucky to have escaped with his life. The waters did abate and near the bridge they had fallen to about thirty inches within twenty four hours but all low lying houses remained water logged for some time afterwards and much furniture was ruined. The cottagers here were rescued by boats in conditions that were often fraught with danger from fast flowing flood waters carrying debris. In the waterlogged fields the hay and corn crops had suffered to such an extent that much of it was left in a hopeless condition. There had been a heavy toll among the poultry of the region but most of the livestock appeared to have been removed to safety without loss or had managed to find their way onto higher ground and huddle together for warmth and comfort.

WENSUM VALLEY

This beautiful area presented a tragic appearance, large areas of the countryside were under water, bridges had been swept away and the rescue of livestock by boat was no mean feat of achievement. The railway bridge at **Lenwade** sunk and necessitated the stoppage of railway traffic, while at **Lyng** and Whitwell the railway bridges completely collapsed. The total losses in the valley were estimated to amount to around £4,000.

WEYBOURNE

A cottage built over a disused well had its floor covering give way and a nearly new piano, chiffonier, table, chairs and other furniture tumbled into the hole.

WINTERTON

Two cottages occupied by Messrs. Hodds and Chenery had the gable ends blown out and other damage done by the heavy rains flooding into the rooms of the cottages.

WYMONDHAM

Many stranded passengers spent Monday, Tuesday and Wednesday at Wymondham, on Monday night it was estimated as many as seven hundred people were stranded in the town, their piles of luggage piled up on Wymondham station becoming a pitiable sight to behold. The plight of the passengers stranded here was made worse by the station being cut off from the town after the Tiffey, a stream that normally burbled its way through the town, rose several feet above the surface of the roadway. It was rendered impossible to reach provision shops and the like owing to the bridge at the foot of the hill being impassable and it was here on Monday evening young Mr Laycock (son of Mr C. J. Laycock, provision merchant, was coming into the town driving a cart containing some fat pigs, the result was the horse, cart, pigs and Laycock and another youth were carried away by the current. Both horse and pigs were drowned and Laycock had a very narrow escape. He was carried by the stream and it was a small wonder he managed

DAMGATE BRIDGE. WYMONDHAM. AFLOOD. AUG. 1912.

Little was left of Damgate bridge at Wymondham.

to escape from drowning. Later, one side of the Bridge was swept away and the road torn up. Drain pipes were swirled about like straws and the water spread for a great distance.

The GER Wymondham and Dereham line had a bridge washed away near Cemetery Lane. The brickwork was washed away and all that remains over the twelve foot space are rails with the sleepers still attached to them. The road bridge at this spot also suffered damage and the surrounding land took on the appearance of a lake with sheds floating upon it. The row of houses in Cemetery Lane were also flooded to a depth of two feet on the ground floors.

Most of the roadway to The Lizard, reached from the town by passing under a bridge near the station, was washed away and deposited about twenty yards away and an iron gulley cover was carried along by the force of water for several yards. The waters here also undermined the bridge and immediate attention was necessary to save the structure.

TIFFEY BRIDGE WYMONDHAM

Tiffey Bridge overflowed by flood waters, Wymondham.

Town Green, Wymondham,
26 August 1912.

Bread delivery to stranded
householders, Pople Street,
Wymondham

The waters abated and
revealed the damage
inflicted upon the Tiffey
Bridge, Wymondham

The house of Mr. George Stubbs near the bridge suffered terribly, the water reaching the tops of the downstair windows and a great number of fowl were drowned here.

A short distance away the bridge over what was usually a small stream that ran under the Norwich and London main line had gone and part of the embankment had slipped onto the rails.

Water and flooding was present to varying degrees in all the principal streets of Wymondham. On the Downham Road another bridge collapsed. At the moment of this calamity a wagon and three horses were passing over and the vehicle vanished into the water. The horses were released by cutting the traces and thus they escaped drowning. Trees fell on the Norwich Road, some of them tearing down telegraph wires as they did so.

The flues flooded at the gas works and the fires were almost extinguished but thanks to continuous pumping from about 1.30pm until 9.00pm the gas supply was maintained for the town. It proved impossible to work in the gravel pits as they were all flooded and large numbers of the men employed there were left out of work for some time afterwards. The flood waters disappeared quickly and by Thursday the worst of the water was gone.

Lizard Bridge, Wymondham.

Further into the town, the most serious damage was suffered in Damgate Street. It is near here some old houses that overlooked the stream were in danger from immediate fall and the residents were advised to clear out at once. After a long delay a start was made to move the furniture and effects but it was too late and the building, complete with contents collapsed into the water. Fortunately no-one was hurt.

YARMOUTH AND GORLESTON

The steamer *Egyptian* went down on the Scroby Sands off Yarmouth, the thirty three members of the crew were all saved by the Gorleston lifeboat Elizabeth Simpson but it was impossible to salvage her, as the tugs could not get near enough. The crew's effects have been brought ashore, with the captain's dog and canary, but by the Customs regulations the dog had to be placed in quarantine as the *Egyptian* came from Antwerp.

Gale force winds blew from the north-east across the town and a deluge of rain fell until noon on Monday. The wind then eased only to swing round to west-north-west and returned with a hurricane-like blast from about 1.00pm until the early evening. It was with the coming of this stronger storm accompanied by torrents of rain that flooded many of the streets, shops and houses and caused the most disruption and damage in the town. The beach was deserted, as were the streets save a few hardy souls in oilies braving the elements. The trams did a roaring trade, many of them displaying 'full inside' but by the evening the trams were stopped on several routes owing to floods and obstructions. Large trees were torn up by the storm in many parts of the town. At about 4.00pm a large tree near St Mary's Church in Southtown was blown down breaking the tramway wires and demolishing part of the churchyard wall as it fell. As a consequence of the damage caused by this fallen tree the tramway service between Yarmouth and Gorleston was suspended for the rest of the day. In other areas houses were damaged, windows were blown out and the streets and rows became smattered with debris of all descriptions.

A serious situation developed on the Lichfield Estate at Southtown where there were hundreds of small houses. Similar floods occurred in many other parts of the town. On all sides distressed householders were busily engaged in baling out their premises, water rose in basements and rain penetrated many roofs and even brick walls. A distresses landlady in Havelock Road had a house full of summer visitors who decided to change their quarters as upon going upstairs they found pools of water on their beds. The next door neighbour volunteered to take them in and the offer was accepted. Pleased with her unexpected good fortune in securing her neighbours' lodgers the landlady went to show the new arrivals their rooms and found, to her chagrin, her beds were in much the same condition as her neighbour! In another instance a house in one of the rows that was full of visitors had five out of six rooms rendered uninhabitable through the intrusion of water. It was observed that the majority of households had basins, tins and other receptacles placed around the house and tin baths had to be placed on beds to catch the drops.

Notwithstanding the gale on Monday the *Yarmouth Belle* Steamer ran as usual and just managed to get through to Yarmouth, arriving shortly after 9.00pm. She had an extremely rough passage and the few passengers who braved the journey 'had enough of it' when she arrived. The steamer had considerable difficulty in making the Harbour and in her first attempt the force of the gale almost blew her to the South Pier but the captain put her about and proceeded to the Roads where he took a much wider sweep and ran for the harbour. This time he was more successful but after the steamer had crossed the bar the gale carried her broadside onto the South Pier where she got hung up but fortunately no damage was done. Ropes were got out and she was hauled along the side of the pier to the bend where her bows were swung out and she proceeded up the river.

The *Yarmouth Belle* was not so fortunate on Wednesday when she was lying near Hall Quay and the Norwegian steamer *Agusta* was carried by the strong ebb tide from where she was lying by the Haven Bridge on to the *Belle* causing some considerable damage.

Fishing boats that returned to Yarmouth on Thursday 29 August bore many marks of the storm. All had lost most of their sails and only got back with difficulty. There is some anxiety for those not yet reported. The crew has been rescued from a Belgian trawler wrecked on the Haisborough Sands, but her name has not been transmitted.

At **Gorleston** all the low-lying streets were flooded to the degree they were impassable, Leighton Pierrot Pavilion was completely wrecked and a small house near the Half Way House was blown down.

ON THE BROADS

At Surlingham Ferry, Coldham Hall, Buckenham Ferry and other riverside resorts from Norwich to Oulton there was three feet of water in many houses. Chickens, pigs and domestic pets were drowned in their hundreds. Enterprising broadsmen did not let the edible birds go to waste and were soon selling dressed fowls at a shilling each.

One gentleman attempted to spend the night in his yacht at **Whitlingham**. Mooring well out, he thought he would ride the flood waters but at four in the morning he found his yacht had driven ashore but he had no means of reaching terra firma. He sent up cries for help but could make no-one hear and was at last forced to wade through the waters on the marshes neck deep. **Hoveton** suffered flooding when the river overflowed and **Wroxham Bridge** was shaking and swaying at the shock of the thudding water. The whole pile of heavy masonry would have been swept away hours before had not the river burst at another spot a little lower down and roared off in tens of thousands of tons down a by-road to make a river and that before it flooded a tremendous acreage under the shadow of Wroxham old church. At **Horning** a dozen yachts were 'shored off' the bowling green at the Swan and Ferry Inns. At **Ludham** Bridge, the river had flowed right across the

The floods at Hoveton.

Horning Ferry under flood. A number of yachts were 'shored off' the bowling green here.

roadways and it was impossible to get under the archway of the bridge in any kind of craft. All round **Potter Heigham** was like a great lake; sailing dinghies were navigated where a few days previously cattle had been grazing in their hundreds. All of the bungalows from the bridge to Kendal Dyke were isolated and all the boatbuilders' yards were deluged and slipways, masts, boats and all sorts of gear floated away. Three bullocks on the flooding marshes were driven into a dyke by the encroaching flood waters and were drowned. On the ebb tide such a quantity of material piled up against Acle Bridge concerns were raised that the bridge would be swept away too, but fortunately it stood firm though the torrents.

On Monday the Annual meeting of the Yarmouth and Gorleston Angler's Association was being held at the Sportsmans' Arms at Ormesby St Michael and a large number of members were present. Waiting out the storms of the morning, the weather got finer and it was decided to commence the competitions for the usual prizes. Accordingly, at 1.00pm the competitors set off from the staithe in their boats. An hour later the storm broke and concerns were raised to the fate of the crews. Hour after hour passed but none returned until two or three half drowned members reached the inn. They reported they had run the boats as near ashore as they could for the reeds and then waded ashore. Mr. W. Richmond at once organised a search party and succeeded in rescuing many members from the half-swamped boats. Mr Mobbs was got out of his boat in a very exhausted state and had to be carried to the inn, where restoratives were applied. It was a bad experience for all but few would ever forget their outing in 1912.

THE RAILWAYS AND THE FLOOD

It was stated in the press that the railways had never suffered so much as during the floods of August 1912.

ON THE GREAT EASTERN RAILWAY

Passengers on the train from Swaffham to Norwich noticed the first signs of flooding close to Yaxham Station, further along they saw corn fields where the shocks of corn appeared just over the water. The 9.50am Liverpool Street to Cromer train steamed into the storm shortly after leaving London. The weather conditions made the conditions very hard going for the train, it was compelled to stop or go slow on a number of occasions but the crew were determined to carry on. At Forncett the driver waded through three feet of water under the engine to protect the fire box with tarpaulins lest it would not have been able to proceed. The train reached Swainsthorpe where, a delay of two hours and ten minutes had to be made due to the line being flooded and the earthwork under many sleepers being washed away. The train was eventually taken through by an alternative route into Wymondham where a voluntary collection was made by passengers for the driver and fireman as a mark of appreciation of their courage and devotion to duty. The train eventually set off for Norwich via Hethersett, on this leg of the journey the railway line was submerged and the train had to run through water from the hundreds of little cuts from the coppices and lands that were pouring water onto the line. At one point close to Hethersett the water was so deep that volumes of steam rose up from the engine and it was as much as the engine could do to pull through. The train eventually arrived at Thorpe Station at 3.30pm (some three hours late) but the state of the lines out of Norwich to Cromer and North Walsham prevented the train from completing its journey and the passengers were accommodated in the first class waiting room until cabs were provided to Whitlingham so they might get on the Cromer line.

Part of the line at Flordon, between Norwich and Ipswich was washed away and no traffic between Norwich and Ipswich was possible after 10am. The Waveney Valley line was under water while serious flooding occurred on the line between Norwich and Lowestoft and the services between Norwich and Cromer, Wroxham and County School, Wymondham and Dereham were all suspended.

Traffic on all three lines out of Great Yarmouth was suspended on Monday afternoon. Anxious passengers making enquiries at the Southtown and Vauxhall Stations were

Great Eastern Railway freight train comes to grief at Barsham Bridge where the flood swollen waters of the river Stiffkey swept away the bridge supports on 26 August 1912.

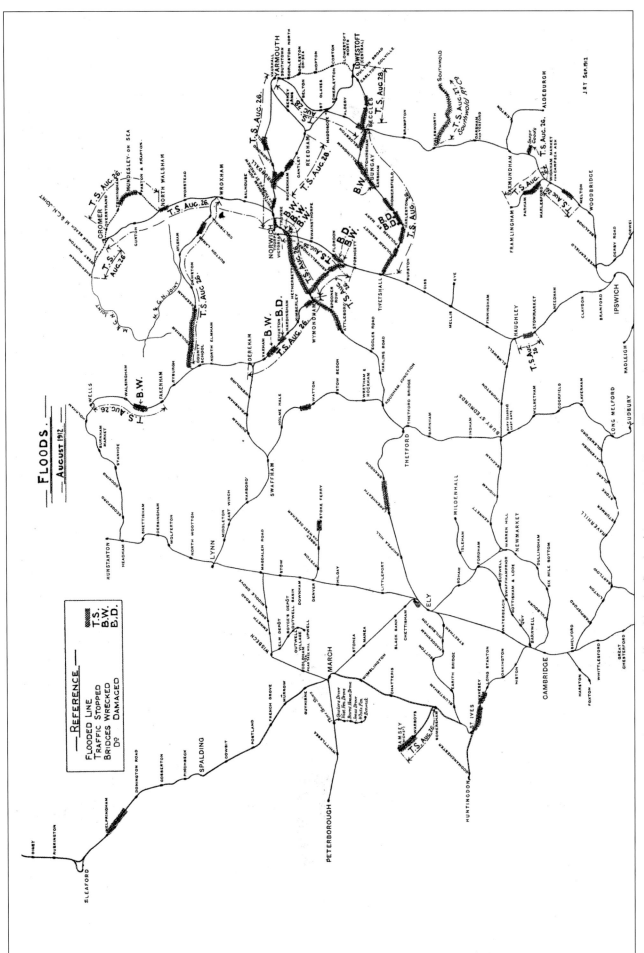

Map of the areas of the Great Eastern Railway network affected by the floods of August 1912 (*Roger Kingstone*)

invariably told 'If you want to get there you will have to get a taxi'. One of the greatest inconveniences was the landslip at Postwick, between Whitlingham and Brundall , that stopped all trains from Yarmouth to Norwich, by both the Acle and Reedham routes and in consequence the service from Vauxhall Station was entirely suspended after the 11.55 train from Yarmouth to Norwich had passed. On Tuesday a local service from Yarmouth to Brundall was established via Reedham and back every two hours, and a local service from Lowestoft to Reedham was established in connection with it.

The Great Northern evening express from King's Cross to Cromer, Yarmouth and other East Coast towns containing many holiday and business passengers was stopped at King's Lynn. The passengers, many of them families with children, were deposited with their luggage upon a flooded platform and after receiving no news of progress were left with no other option than to brave the heavy rain to seek lodgings in the town. Others, such as the day excursionists from Liverpool Street stranded at Yarmouth Southtown Station were more fortunate and about 160 belated passengers ended up sleeping in waiting rooms where they were given tea, coffee, cakes, bread and butter by the station master.

At Wymondham the railway bridge was washed away so the GER arranged to convey passengers to Norwich by char-a-bancs while at Great Yarmouth railway station hundreds of visitors anxious to return home found all the trains cancelled. A great crowd gathered on the platform and those for whom there was room took their seats in the carriages of a train which they hoped would go to London. After a considerable wait they were informed all further trains were cancelled due to subsidence. Many were in a pitiable state having exhausted all their funds on their holidays. The stationmaster lit fires in the waiting rooms and allowed others to sleep in the carriages, also distributing tea and bread and butter among the children.

At midnight the news came that the train could be sent on. Twelve day trippers from Grimston Road, near King's Lynn, left Yarmouth Beach Station where they had been accommodated and fed for four days, not able to pay for lodgings. The guard's room and waiting room were placed at the disposal of the party, which included women and children. They were made comfortable with rugs and supplied by the officials with excellent meals.

Many railway passengers had their journeys disrupted, cancelled or were left stranded. A young lady who started from North Elmham, a distance of about twenty miles from North Walsham on Monday 26 August records her journey as: Left North Elmham 2.43pm, proceeded via East Dereham. On arrival at Yaxham train stopped two and half hours and then returned to East Dereham, there stopped one and a half hours, telegraphed to North Walsham, proceeded to Swaffham and Lynn (half hour stop), then Lynn to Bury, returned to Lynn, the proceeded from Lynn to Newmarket, Ely, Cambridge (stayed half and hour) and arrived Liverpool Street at 4am. Tuesday after a stop of one and half hours, found she could not get to Norwich so went to Yarmouth, arrived South-town Station 9.00am. At 9.30 left Beach Station and arrived at Stalham at 2.30. The journey from Stalham to North Walsham was made by road where she arrived at 4.10pm and all this for a fare of 3s. 2d.

ON THE MIDLAND AND GREAT NORTHERN RAILWAY

There were no less than three blocks on the Midland and Great Northern Railway between Great Yarmouth and Melton Constable. One between Ormesby and Hemsby, another between Horning and Stalham and the third between Corpusty and Melton Constable. The 2.10 from Melton Constable to Great Yarmouth was the last train to arrive at Beach Station before stoppage and the 2.45 for Birmingham, Manchester and the North was the last to successfully leave Yarmouth. This latter train got as far as Aylsham where it was held up for the night. The 1.30pm from Yarmouth for Yorkshire, Lancashire, Derby and Nottinghamshire only got as far as Melton Constable.

About fifty excursionists were stranded on Yarmouth Beach Station but Station Master Coe and his staff did their best to make them as comfortable as possible. The Third Class Waiting Room, the Ladies' Waiting Room, the Guard's Room and railway carriages were all placed at their disposal. Here they slept at night and received three meals daily – kippers for breakfast, fried fish for lunch and bread, butter, jam or marmalade for tea.

Effecting repairs on the
Midland and Great
Northern Railway after
the floods of August
1912.

The branch line from North Walsham to Mundesley suffered much damage, tons of earth from one side of the embankment slipped, leaving the rails and sleepers suspended. Further down the line the sides of a cutting slipped and earth completely covered the rails. A landslip at Barney Bank, three and a half miles on the Yarmouth side of Fakenham caused great disruption, interrupting all traffic on that line and it was only on Tuesday that a local service between Yarmouth and Stalham was started again from the Beach Station and a run was made as far as North Walsham on Wednesday.

COUNTING THE COST

At a meeting of Norfolk County Council on Saturday 31 August, County Surveyor Mr Heslop presented a report on damage suffered by the roads and bridges across the county. The damage had been almost entirely confined to the eastern division of the county. Where the approach roads were low the damage to the structure had been inconsiderable, the flood water having a free flow. No bridge erected by the County Council had given way; Mr Heslop estimated £15,800 would cover the damage to bridges and culverts, No bridge

The remnants of the bridge at Itteringham 27 August 1912.

Clearing up the wooden bricks road displaced by the flooding on Duke Street, Norwich.

in the Acle district had been destroyed but in the Aylsham district twenty-two bridges had been damaged or destroyed. Bridges had been destroyed at Spixworth, Hevingham, Ingworth, Saxthorpe, Itteringham, Banningham, St Faith's, Colby, Gunton, Coltishall, King's Beck, Alburgh, Thurgarton, Erpingham and Brampton Beck. In the Dereham district nine bridges and culverts were destroyed. There were five in Harling district, eight each in Walsingham and Wymondham districts and one each in Castle Acre, Docking and Downham districts.

A rough estimate for the restoration of the roads was placed at £12,000 and it was pointed out that it was of the utmost importance that they should be open to traffic as soon as possible. Mr Heslop proposed to erect temporary timber bridges to carry loads up to two tons. The report was adopted and it was decided to make application to the Road Board for assistance to meet the burden cast upon the county and to apply to the Local Government Board for leave to borrow such further sums necessary to complete the repairs.

Dutch Workmen in Wet Weather Costume, Cantley.   No. J. & S. 7378

It had been a wet season and the weather delayed work on the Cantley sugar beet factory but the Dutch workmen brought over to grow the beet in the fields carried on regardless.

The Horsey Breach 1938

ON THE NIGHT OF Saturday 12 February 1938 a vicious north westerly gale whipped up across the sea and drove high waves against the sand hills of the east Norfolk coast. The high tide at Horsey was 10 feet above the Newlyn datum, 7 feet higher than an ordinary spring tide and the heavy seas washed away the marram that covered face of the bank. Horsey is only 8ft 11ins above sea level and very soon the waves were overlapping the defences and as the water ran off on the landward side it cut deep runnels that further weakened the bank. Soon after the tide began to ebb, at about 7.00pm, a length of 517 yards of the dunes at Horsey collapsed and water rushed through the new breach flooding 7500 acres of low-lying hinterland. The force of water was so strong that it carried away chicken sheds, outbuildings and swept away gates, fence posts, stacks of hay and reeds and even wooden bridge that was carried about three quarters of a mile away and was only stopped by a belt of trees.

Map of the flooded area of Horsey and District by J. E. G. Mosby, 1938

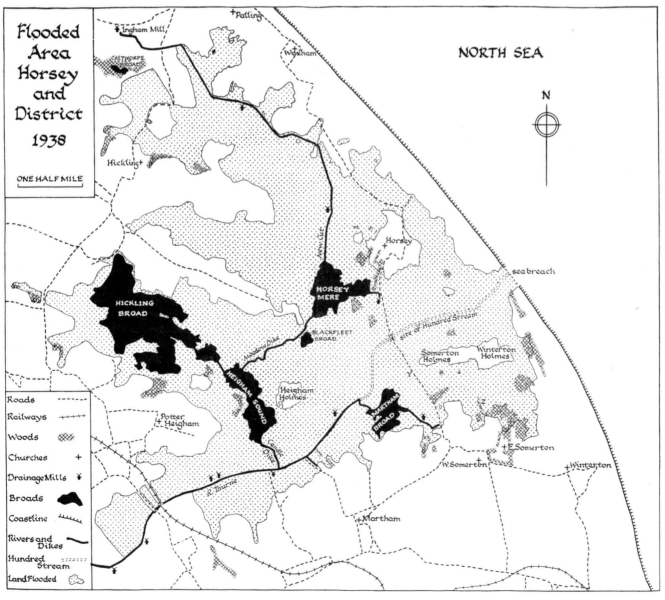

Aerial photograph showing
the flood plain over many
acres of farm land and
broad after the sea breach
at Horsey 1938

Roy Randell's car
surrounded by flood
waters on Horsey Road

Roy Randell (*Paul Randell*)

Water thundered across the marshes and sea and broad merged as one. Horsey village was inundated and a complete area of fifteen square miles of neighbouring villages, farms and marshes were flooded. A number of Horsey residents made to the sand hills fearing they were their only hope feared for their lives as they made their way over two miles while the sea 'rushed behind them like a great river.' Several villages were evacuated, it was amazing nobody was killed by the flood but many livestock were lost in the inundation. One man, however, had a very narrow escape. Roy Randell, a 24 year old milk roundsman of Horsey gave a number of interviews about his experience at the time, but a letter written by Roy as he was recuperating to one of the medical personnel who had attended to him after his experience, concerned 'you should not believe all you read in the London papers,' he tells the story in his own words and is published here for the first time:

'*Dear Nurse Fuller*

Thank you very much for your letter and cigs. It is very kind of you to remember me. Yes, I had a terrible time but am recovering very well. Dr. Rochford was satisfied this morning but said I must stay in bed a day or two yet...Now let me try and explain what happened. I had finished my rounds and started off home about 7pm. I had got past the

Above left: The height of
the waters at Somerton - a
dislodged chicken house is
in the background.

Above right: View of the
council houses from the
Nelson Inn at Horsey

*rump on Horsey Road bout not to the Hundred Stream when suddenly the water flew up
over the car. I thought the radiator had burst. Then the engine stopped. I scrambled out to
find the water up top my thighs and a terrible current making it impossible for me to wade
back to Somerton. I managed to get back into the car, by this time the water had risen to
5ft and I had to lie on the top of the seat hoping for the best. I was afraid the car would
be swept into the dyke, but it didn't move many feet. I had to keep my eyes fixed on a tree
all night. All went well until high tide 5.30 Sunday morning when the old sea came over
again with greater force. Huge waves swept over the top of the car and smashed the
windows. I tore the top off the car and scrambled out. When day broke my hopes were
raised as I felt certain someone would search for me. I could see hundreds of cars and
people on the Martham Road. I waved my coat but somebody seemed to see it. Then an
aeroplane came over me twice, but he passed by and I gave up hope and prepared myself
for death and eternity. I did not feel afraid as I had been praying all the time. My chief
concern was for those I loved. About half an hour later I saw an object at the Somerton
end of the road and to my relief found it was a boat. Imagine my feelings if you can. Then
tree more appeared. At last I was rescued and taken to home where I am having every
attention possible. Everyone is so kind...'*

Roy was eventually rescued shortly after midday on Sunday by a rescue team headed by
the well-known Broads boats owner Mr. Herbert Woods of Potter Heigham. Woods
followed the route of the Old Hundred Stream knowing that it would have been the only
route by which a boat could pass over the Thurne river wall to the flooded road where the
car was caught.

Randell had waved his coat because he had been too hoarse, through exhaustion, to
shout. Rowing past submerged farm buildings Woods' boat hurried to the car. Two other
boats had also spotted him and were on their way too: one containing Roy's brothers
Robert and Burdy, the other Mr. C.T. A. Beevor and PC Jenkins of Winterton. The Woods
boat reached Roy first and helped him aboard. At the time of rescue it was noted the roof
of the car was only about a foot and a half above the flood water.

Mrs. Skipper of the Manor House in the Warren, Horsey gave her account of the night
to *a Yarmouth Mercury* reporter:

*'Our house is hardly 200 yards from the sand hills and yet we only had a few minutes
warning. My grocery man, Mr. Cator of Somerton, had gone back to his van to fetch the
goods I had just ordered when I heard him shout, come quickly, the water is coming in!'
He had found his van trapped by the sea and when I rushed out I saw the water in the road
and things beginning to float. My husband and I and my niece Rita threw on our coats and
made a dash for the sand hills, with Mr. Cator and our three dogs. As we went I could see
the sea pouring over the marshes and racing us. In my hurry I tore my mackintosh climbing
over a gate, but in the end we got to the hills in time. We knew they would be high and we
were able to walk along to Waxham, where we got a lift to Palling. My husband carried
our ferrets on his back and brought them safely through. Now we are staying at the inn
here, thanks to the kindness of Mr. W. Hamblin.'*

The Waxham and Palling Road under flood.

Mr Robert Nichols was living at the northern end of Waxham when the floods came. His housekeeper recalled hearing the noise of a car outside and that it was only when Mr Nichols went outside they discovered the sea was in their garden. They quickly pulled on rubber boots and the car took them to Palling. Doors were no barrier to the flood and as the level rose in downstairs rooms families fled to upper floors as several feet of water entered homes and crept slowly up the bottom flights of stairs. About fifty children and a hundred adults were rescued from Horsey in lorries and boats. The evacuation effort began with Mr J. R. Bensley of Martham who had called at the Nelson Inn to take a darts team to Little Ormesby. His drive along the tree-lined coast road at around 6.45pm had seemed like nothing too out of the ordinary but when her arrived at the pub he was told the team he had come to collect had not all turned up and while he was talking to the people in the bar the sound of running feet were heard, the door burst open and white-faced tenants from new houses in the street rushed in crying 'The sea is in our houses!' The men determined to get the woman and children out first and ran from place to place collecting villagers and directing them to Mr. E. G. King's farm on the higher ground. Some packed into one of Mr King's lorries and were taken through the waters to Waxham. It was a terrifying journey for the women and children. With gulleys and dips hidden by the ever-rising water, the road was full of treachery. The tricky light of the moon threw deceptive shadows to increase the peril.

Their journeys were blighted when one lorry got as far as Delf's farm when the engine succumbed and the men had to push it back to the farm and transfer the passengers. To get to Waxham Road a foot-track that had to be crossed provided a tricky obstacle. Time after time the whirling water got into the engines but the work carried on.

Other villages crowded into Mr. Bensley's bus and soon there was a constant – if frequently delayed - service between Horsey and the point nearly two miles away on the Palling road where the flood had stopped and a fleet of private cars driven by residents from miles around waited to take the evacuated to Sea Palling where the Village Hall acted as a reception centre. Here, villagers waited to offer assistance and temporary homes for those flooded out. By Sunday morning nearly all those who had been rescued had been taken in by these good Samaritans, while others managed to stay with relatives.

When the rescue work became impossible the men snatched a meal and what sleep they could before the dawn. As the grey light filtered over the scene it revealed the full magnitude of the flood for the first time. It seemed incredible that when daylight had last left the land it had been a patchwork of fields and cottages. The men rose and set off in their rescue efforts again. Three boats were loaded onto Mr. King's lorry at Palling and launched on the flooded road, up which the flood waters had crept during the night. The water now separated them from the people still in the village for a distance or nearly two miles, but

to get there they had to cover at least a mile more, leaving the road further along for open fields. Hidden obstacles threatened the bottom of the boats as they glided along and their route had to be chosen with great care. Quick reckonings were made to check who had been left in the flooded area in the night and one by one the outlying homes were accounted for.

Once in the village, our gallant band of rescuers and other brave rescue parties found people very grateful to be helped to evacuate, clambering down through the upper storey windows of their homes into the waiting rescue boats while a few hardy souls, although thankful for the gesture, refused to leave their homes as they concerned for their livestock.

Many feared the danger was not over on Sunday. Fears were voiced that the flood waters could penetrate as far inland as Norwich. Potter Heigham was also considered a danger point as flood water began to find its way down the river Bure, through Hickling, Horsey and Martham Broads. The flow of water was considerably constricted at the old Potter Heigham bridge and the water went over the walls on the Martham side of the river near Potter and many riverside bungalows and houses were inundated. Further afield the sea came over the bank at Heacham and flooded the low lying land. The storm swept Cromer pier with the highest seas recorded for forty years carrying away and damaging a number of beach huts on the promenade. Houses were flooded at Cley and

Above left: The floods near the Mill House (left) at Horsey

Above right: Mr A. A. Francis, the Martham photographer who recorded many of the scenes of the Horsey floods is seen here, tripod under arm as he wades along the Waxham Road.

Horse drawn transports evacuating people and animals from the Horsey area. (*Paul Randell*)

Flooding near the Staithe, Hickling with Edgar Gibbs's lorry and Beales's Garage in the background.

boats were used in the streets. Tide boards were set up in doorways to keep out the water but proved ineffective as the floods rose to over 4ft there. The Cromer to Wells road was flooded to a depth of between two and three feet in places. At Salthouse the marshes flooded and the road immersed. Many roads were blocked by fallen trees and telephone wires were brought down. Breydon Water overflowed its banks and flooded the Burgh Castle Marshes, trees were blown down in the Fleggs, the Yarmouth sea wall survived the pounding and held the angry waters back and gave save harbour to two exhausted steamer crews who had only narrowly reached it after terrifying ordeals on the gale-ridden North Sea.

As boats restored communication with Horsey on Sunday the stories of disaster to livestock filtered through. Pigs and chickens had a high mortality, a number of cattle also suffered and horses were found drowned at Somerton. In Horsey Church, standing high and dry in a parish of water, the Rector, Rev. R. G.K. Hart, conducted morning service for a congregation of one. Sightseers flocked to the edges of the flooded area on Sunday too. Cars and cycles were described as 'thickly parked' and as more sightseers came over the ensuing days as the story hit the national media some made the trip from as far away as London and the first traffic jam in the history of the village occurred at Martham!

Below left: Russell Brooks (right) and a pal find penny farthings the ideal height to cycle through the flood waters.

Below right: Visitors to see the Horsey floods cause the first ever traffic jam in the village of Martham.

On Monday 14 February another in-rush of water came from the sea breach during the morning's high tide threatening Hickling. Sandbags placed across the road near the Broad saved several cottages from being cut off. It was also a day for taking stock of the situation.

On Tuesday 15 February a livestock rescue party was organised by PC Bailey of Hickling, a man who had worked tirelessly to help people in the rural community since the inundation, and Inspector Brehany of the RSPCA, who had arrived by motor boat. With Mr. F. D. Starling of Street Farm Horsey, Cecil Beales, Mr. T. Dyball, Mr. R. King and Mr. R. Randell they set out in two small boats; one was a rowing boat, the other had a small outboard motor, to rescue some horses on Horsey Island. The rescue was hindered by high winds and one of the boats was almost upset when it was dashed against the side of the partially submerged shelter where the horses had been up to their bellies since the inundation. The horses were frightened and getting them out of the shelter was no mean feat. Once they were out the job was to shepherd them to safety. This was accomplished with the two boats driving them towards an island of dry land around Starling's farmhouse. The rescue took nearly five hours but it brought seven fine colts to safety. It was still only possible to reach Horsey Island at low tide by walking thigh deep along a lane from the Warren near the sand hills. A reporter made the journey found the thirty inhabitants 'calm and unperturbed' by the waters that swirled around them.

Farmer Starling with a mare and her foal that were among the horses he and a gallant rescue team drove to dry land from the floods. (*Martham Local History Group*)

Once all who wished to be evacuated had been transported from the floods, the task of rescuing animals began. Here, cart loads of pigs and their rescue parties are being carted to dry land.

This tractor and reaper had been submerged but when the flood water abated it was recovered, the magnetos were dried, the engine started and covered with a tarpaulin to keep the water out the tractor was driven away.

Unloading rescued cattle at Walnut Farm, Waxham

The total area flooded was 7469 acres and the distance along the outside margin 43 miles. The task of draining off the water from the flooded levels was stupendous for the majority of the volume had to be pumped out the marshes into the higher level of the river Thurne, or into the New Cut and its connecting dikes, Meadow Dike and Candle Dike. The progress of this operation was impeded by the lack of gradient in the rivers and by the roundabout way the water had to travel to reach the only outlet at Yarmouth. The flood water was drained off at the Martham Level in 28 days. During this time the drainage pump was working continuously day and night. Fortunately this level was not affected by the second inundation. It took sixteen weeks to clear the level east of Candle Dike. After they had been drained the marshes looked desolate in the extreme. Instead of fresh green the eye was greeted by a dismal rust-red. The trees were killed, even the insects exterminated and thousands of fish in the broads and the rivers died. The East

Recovering a drowned farm animal at Somerton

Building a new defence across the breach at Horsey, February 1938

Norfolk River Catchment Board assessed the damage at the time to about £13,000 in Horsey alone.

Immediate steps were taken to repair the breach but this was not without danger to the workmen. On 1 March 1938 about a hundred extra men had been drafted in to help in the sand bag piling operation to close the breach. At high tide the ground upon which they were working flooded and Horsey man Tom Fuller was drawn into the mud and had to be pulled by his workmates to higher ground. A crane also had to be dragged to safety as water encircled it and several horses had to be rescued as the waters approached. The work did resume and by the end of March a 7ft barrier of bags filled with sand and clay placed behind a line of wooden piles had been erected across the whole length of the gap. High enough to keep out the highest ordinary tide on 3 April a north westerly gale with a velocity of 50-70 miles per hour produced waves that washed over the new defences at high tide. The battering was so severe that nearly all of the new built defences, piles, sandbags and the light railway that had run along the top of the barrier were swept inland. The subsequent flooding was not as extensive as that of February and no fresh ground was affected.

After the second breach in April The East Norfolk River Catchment Board consulted the borough engineers at Lowestoft and Great Yarmouth, both of whom had long experience in combating coastal erosion and appointed Mr. S. W. Mobbs, the then borough engineer

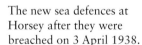

The new beach defences at Horsey

The new sea defences at Horsey after they were breached on 3 April 1938.

Topping off the new sea defences completed at Horsey, April 1938. *(Paul Randell)*

Horsey Drainage Mill may be seen here under flood but the mill did sterling work helping to pump off thousands of gallons of water in the aftermath of the inundation.

of Lowestoft, as their engineer. On his recommendation permanent protection work in the form of a barrier of sand hills was begun on a length of coast extending 4½ miles with the Horsey breach rather nearer the north end than the middle.

The work of filling the breach at Horsey was completed in five weeks. The method adopted was to create a dam with sloping faces, 26ft wide at the base and 9ft in height, composed of concrete-filled sandbags on each face with a sand-bagged core. The bank was

The view from the mill at
Somerton looking towards
the broad.

constructed in three layers, each encased in steel meshing and with the concrete bags further
held together by steel rods driven through the layers of bags. The immediate area of the
breach was also fitted with a system of groynes, running out to the sea for about 400ft.
Their purpose being to collect 'littoral drift' to assist the beach to re-form where it has
been washed away by the action of the waves. The total cost of the coastal defence works
was estimated at £432,975 and was completed in December 1938. It took months for the
rust brown sludge and tide lines on properties and countryside to be removed or fade. The
fish at Hickling, Horsey Mere and Heigham Sound and in their surrounding area had been
killed by the inundation. Parts of the broads were rendered 'semi- salt water lakes' and
millions of shrimps appeared in them. It would be months before the waters recovered
and years for the farm land to recover its viability for cultivation.

Above left: Fish killed by
the salt water at Martham.

Above right: Farmland
shortly after the majority
of flood waters had been
drained off. It would be
years before this land
would be restored to
cultivation. *(Paul Randell)*

The 1953 Floods

THE NIGHT OF SATURDAY 31 January 1953 was a night of extreme weather conditions. Floods smashed into the East Coast, torrential rain fell and winds howled across the land wreaking havoc, death and disaster. That fateful night also provoke incredible acts of selfless heroism from members of the emergency services, US and British servicemen and very much in the spirit of Dunkirk and the Blitz, extraordinary acts of heroism and kindness were to be found during and after the flood disaster from ordinary people. From Lincolnshire to Kent, long stretches of Britain's most vulnerable coastline had been rendered unrecognisable as the sea breached defences in 1,400 locations. Three hundred and seven people were drowned along with thousands of cattle, sheep, horses, poultry and domestic pets. Twenty four thousand five hundred houses were damaged and 40,000 people were evacuated over the ensuing days. Over 150,000 acres of land, much of it prime agricultural quality, was deluged with salt water that rendered the countryside a horrible rusty brown tint for months afterwards and left the ground sterile for a season or more afterwards.

Often the most disturbing retrospective thoughts of those directly affected by the floods are a sort of shell-shocked disbelief that these events could have happened at all in modern times: the lack of any advance warning for the meteorological office, the speed with which the floods hit the coast and the lack of an efficient and co-ordinated flood warning system along the North Norfolk Coast. To understand why this situation arose one must first consider the lack of technical advances in weather prediction at the time.

In the 1950s weather forecasting was a far cry from the satellite and computer technology available to weather forecasters today. Weather reporting and prediction was based on returns from weatherships, volunteer weather reporting ships, Royal Navy and Merchant ships, aircraft, airfields, lighthouses, coastguards and even enthusiastic amateurs. Collated at Met Office headquarters in Dunstable weather charts were produced at six-hour intervals and delivered to the public via BBC radio; live weather forecasts did not begin on the television until 1954.

The origins of the storm which brought the floods to the East Coast can be traced back to 29 January 1953 and what appeared to be a negligible weather depression of low crossing the Atlantic, which had broken away from the existing low pressure area north of the Azores. Its presence was detected and reported by the merchant vessel *Consuto*, one of the Met Office's volunteer weather reporting ships. *Consuto* sent its report from a bearing south-west of Iceland to the eighth floor offices of the Air Ministry's Metrological Offices in London, who passed the information on for collection at Met Office headquarters in Dunstable. Forecasters did not see this weather feature as out of the ordinary or as particularly significant; it was not even considered strong enough to reach Britain, so they marked it on their charts as a secondary depression and christened it 'Low Z.'

It was not evident until some hours later, when the forecasters received messages from *Weather Explorer*, their official weather reporting ship in the area, which sent reports every three hours. It was soon apparent that Low Z had moved fast, some 350 miles in six hours, and was intensifying. The position was not seen as vitally serious and the expectations were, at worst, of high winds affecting northern Scotland and the Shetlands. Met Office HQ issued the routine response of a normal gale warning.

In the early hours of Friday 30 January the depression was just off Iceland and still not seen as threatening but by noon the depression Low Z had deepened dramatically and was heading south eastwards down over the North Sea. At 6.00pm weather ships were

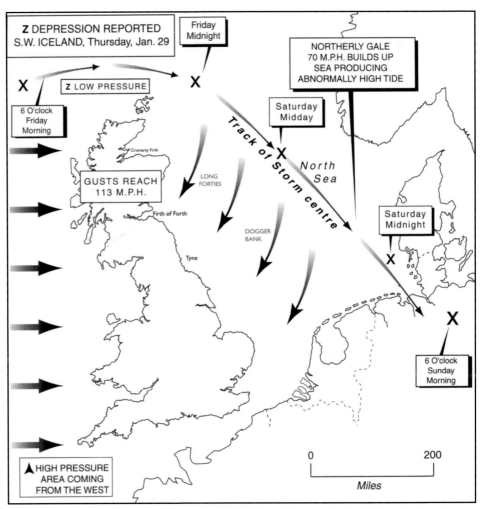

Map charting the progress of Low Z from 29 January to 1 February 1953

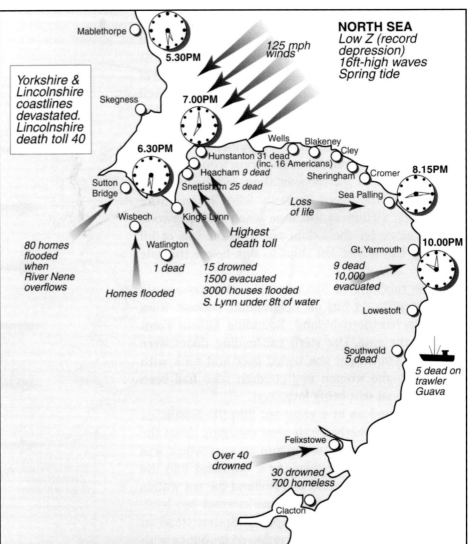

Progress of the East Coast Flood on the night of 31 January 1953

reporting winds of gale force and the edge of the gale had already reached the Shetlands and Faroes. The depression moved steadily on followed by a vast area of high pressure atmosphere stretching from Greenland down the eastern Atlantic to the North African coast.

Low Z was now the centre of roaring gales. At RAF Kinloss on the east coast of Scotland the cups of the anemometer were spun round to the unprecedented wind speed of 113 mph. In the space of these few hours more trees were blown down in Scotland than were normally felled in an entire year. The great gale claimed its first victims at this time when the Fleetwood trawler *Michael Griffiths* was swept under the boiling sea with the loss of all fifteen crew, the first of ten ships to sink before the gale had blown itself out.

At approximately 7.45am on Saturday 31 January the six-year-old British Rail car ferry *Princess Victoria* set out on her regular passage from Stranraer in Scotland to Larne in Northern Ireland. Rounding Milleur Point she was hit by the full force of the gale. Her stern car-loading doors were burst open and buckled. After a gallant fight she keeled over and sank with the loss of 133 lives, including all the women and children who had been thrown into the sea when their lifeboat was being launched.

As Saturday progressed Low Z moved on in a great arc into the North Sea and towards the south. Tremendous northerly winds were sweeping down the North Sea, carrying with them the great masses of water into an area which was already suffering from abnormally high spring tides. As it funnelled into the narrower areas of the North Sea between England and Holland the sea waters piled to become a surging wall of water raised 8ft above the normal sea level. During the afternoon of 31 January the shingle spit of Spurn Head in Yorkshire was breached, in mid-afternoon the Tees overflowed its banks with high tide still an hour away. Lincolnshire's low-lying coast caught the full force of the gales and battering waves shortly after sunset. Sea defences crumbled and within minutes the sea was smashing into Lincolnshire coastal settlements and popular holiday resorts. At Grimsby 1,000 people were rendered homeless, four drowned at Saltfleet and huge waves breached the sea wall at Mablethorpe, where many were drowned and the whole town was soon evacuated.

The waters surged on slamming into the dead-end of the Wash with tremendous force, only a little of which was expended in driving up the open mouth of the Great Ouse, sweeping round the coast of East Anglia smashing into coastal towns, villages ports and resorts. Norfolk saw damage all along its coastline from King's Lynn to Great Yarmouth: particular carnage was inflicted upon the brow of the county between Snettisham and Hunstanton where many people lost their lives in the wooden bungalows which were their first homes in the austere times after the Second World War. The waters smashed into these houses and bungalows so fast that most of those who perished had not stood a chance. The death toll would have been far worse if those who acted so bravely and swiftly here had not been so decisive in the rescue of those who survived the initial deluge.

Beyond Norfolk the surging waters battered the Suffolk coast. Lowestoft was lucky to escape without loss of life, an achievement thanks mostly to the newly completed North Sea wall. The wall of water had been stopped but the water still came and over four hundred homes were flooded. Almost forgotten amid the concerns over the flood, the most significant loss from Lowestoft was the trawler *Guava* that foundered without trace during the night of 31 January with the loss of all eleven crew. At Southwold hundreds of tons of shingle was carried over Ferry Road by the waves in an attack on the town from north and south; two elderly sisters, a 39-year-old mother and her child drowned here. The body of a fifth victim was never recovered. At Felixstowe over forty drowned when a prefab housing estate was all but swept away by the deluge.

Driven along ahead of the spring tide and dragged further southwards by the force of Low Z the sea poured into Jaywick and Canvey Island at about 10.00pm, just at the time when many were in bed and had put their lights out. In these darkened wooden bungalows, very similar to those at Hunstanton, there were horrific death tolls. Thirty seven drowned and 7,000 were rendered homeless as the Jaywick housing estate was engulfed by the surging waters. The entire population of Canvey Island, some 11,500 people, had to be evacuated as the whole island ended up flooded; fifty-eight people were drowned here. The images on television, cinema screens and especially in the press of the rescues and relief effort for the people of Jaywick and Canvey Island are unforgettable to anyone who remembers the East Coast floods.

The water rolled on into the Thames estuary pouring through eight breaches in the South Bank, flooding factories, oil refineries, gas and electricity works. Central London caught the tail end of the catastrophe. Water lapped the top of the parapet along Victoria and Chelsea embankments, spilling over at Greenwich, Woolwich and London Bridge. Finally, the waters sated themselves on British shores by flooding large areas of the Kent coastline.

Tragically, this was not to be the end of the horrific storm. Deflected northwards Low Z only dissipated after reeling into Holland and Belgium reclaiming over 495,000 acres of polder country, bursting fifty dykes and claiming a further 2,000 lives.

A NIGHT TO REMEMBER?

By January 1953 Great Britain had improved a great deal in comparison to the austere years immediately after the war. The country was looking forward to better times: only a few items were still subject to rationing, the country was still glowing after the Festival of Britain in 1951 and after the sadness of losing our beloved King in 1952 the country was looking forward to the street parties and celebrations for the coronation of Queen Elizabeth in June 1953. There was even the new phenomena of a top ten listing of pop records. The number one on 30 January 1953 was *Outside of Heaven* by Eddie Fisher and other popular tunes on the phonogram included Perry Como singing *Don't Let the Stars Get in Your Eyes*, Kay Starr with *Come A-Long A-Love* and Jo Stafford's *You Belong to Me*.

In retrospect the day and early evening of 31 January 1953 was unnerving by how ordinary it was. Remembered locally as 'a bit foul' the wind had been blowing hard all day but it was nothing too far out of the way for a rough winter's day in late January. Saturday markets were still held and spectators pulled their coats and scarves a little closer on the touchlines of the local league football matches. Sundown was at 4.47pm and many folk simply went home and settled down for tea and an evening listening to the radio. At around this time on the Light Programme was Song Club featuring the Ipswich Co-operative Girl's Choir and the Wisbech Male Choral Society. People lucky enough to have a television could have children's programmes on and would no doubt be looking forward to such highlights as Donald Houston and Honor Blackman in *Little Red Monkey* followed by Chan Canasta the magician at 9.00pm.

For many, Saturday night meant a night out at public entertainments. Despite the weather many saw no reason why they should not still attend. In village halls whist and beetle drives like those at Wells and Sea Palling went ahead as usual. Most towns in Norfolk had at least one cinema; along the coast they were mostly part of the 'Regal' chain. Those who braved the high winds and rain for a night at 'the flicks' could enjoy such delights as Jack Warner in *Emergency Call* at Holt, Clarke Gable in *Across the Wide Missouri* at Wells and Frankie Laine in *Rainbow Round My Shoulder* at Cromer. Dances and functions were held at venues like Britannia Pier, Great Yarmouth, the Floral Hall in Gorleston and the Sandringham Hotel at Hunstanton.

For those reading Friday's *Eastern Daily Press* some articles were to take on a new and chillingly ironic significance in the light of events to come. The Reverend Noel Boston, colourful rector of East Dereham and notable Norfolk antiquarian had an article published in the *Norfolk Miscellany* column entitled 'Lost Lands' where he explored ancient encroachments of the sea on the East Anglian coastline. A photo feature and article celebrated the second anniversary of the 32nd AA Brigade of the US Army coming to Sculthorpe. The Commanding Officer of the Brigade, Colonel Metticus W. May stated, 'Never had I seen finer relations between the US Army and the civilian population...the local communities have absorbed our men and their families into community life with mutual respect and acceptance of each other.'

KING'S LYNN

The ancient town of King's Lynn had just rounded off a typical winter's market day. Shoppers and tradesmen mingled on their way home, the town cinemas had queues outside and old folks who mainly resided in the terraces in the hollow basin of South Lynn the evening boded nothing more extraordinary than quiet night out of the wind and cold by the fire. Despite the windy weather ladies had new hair-dos under scarves and their partners held on to their hats as they made their way to the Corn Hall for a dinner dance.

Few could have imagined the night that was to ensue. A few locals who knew the waterways of the port were aware of the potential effects of a strong North-Westerly wind which could unnaturally raise the level of the North Sea. The funnel effect of the Wash operates adversely in such conditions and is further aggravated by the traction of the local winds over vast stretches of shallow water. Murmurings were made from those who knew and worked the waters that the "motion of the sea had been strange" and for the previous three days the outgoing tides were "not getting away as they should have done. There was a lot of water still in the river when the incoming tides came in." If anywhere in Norfolk was to be first to know about or suffer from a North Sea surge it would be King's Lynn because it faced North into the great open seascape of The Wash.

At about 5.30pm the Lynn Harbour Master, Captain J. Nicholson was becoming anxious, the water levels had already reached 24ft compared with the predicted high water of 22.9ft at 7.35pm. The top of the tide was a long way off and the Great Ouse, whipped up the gale, was already licking the tops of its banks. In accordance with the flood warning system which had been in operation between the harbour office and the Lynn emergency services since 1950, Captain Nicholson contacted the local police Chief Superintendent Fred Calvert and the flood warning went out in the town after which a standby alert was given to Lynn Fire Service control. It was the best that could be done, but it was too late. The swirling river and its tributaries began to overflow. As the water began to lap over the quayside police cars were touring the threatened districts with loudspeakers. Most of their

A crowd gathers to watch the rising flood waters on the bridge beside the King's Lynn South Gates, early on the evening of 31 January 1953 (*Lynn News*)

warnings were tragically lost in the howl of the wind. In a desperate bid to get the message through to elderly residents policemen walked round South Lynn knocking on doors to give the warning and folks made their way to the presumed safety of their upper rooms.

The first waters to enter King's Lynn came over the dockside near Page Stair Lane at about 6.00pm. At 6.28pm a call was made for Gayton Road Fire Station for them to attend this area where people were trapped by flood waters. The Fire Service Report states: "When the crew arrived they found several persons congregated at the junction of Page Stair Lane and Tuesday Market Place, the wind sending waves against the wall, at the rear of Barclay's Bank, the scene resembling high tide at the seaside." People attending the dance at the Corn Exchange saw the water sweeping into the Tuesday Market Place managed to escape, some even carrying their dancing partners across the swelling waters to dry land but by the time the fire engine proceeded down Page Stair Lane it could only travel about 25 yards before the waters threatened to impeded the functions of the engine. "…at some 10 yards further the water was chest deep, the shorter personnel having water up to their necks. In all nineteen men, women and children were rescued being carried some 40-50 yards through rough waters with depths up to 4ft."

Water from the swollen River Ouse overflowed beyond the boundaries of the Bentinck Dock to reach Estuary Road. Watchman B. Goodbody was on duty at the Shell Depot and recalled "I sat out the storm in my office which was up a flight of steps. I could hear pit props from the wood yards being tossed about like matchsticks and 250 gallon oil drums rattling around in the rushing water." Flood warnings were flashed on cinema screens but even this came too late for some. Filmgoers at the Pilot Cinema on Pilot Street (now John Kennedy Road) had to sit out the flood in the auditorium, the surge of the water being so rapid it was unsafe for them to leave the building before half past two the following morning when they were formally advised it was safe to do so.

The rising water swiftly enveloped the Tuesday Market Place and flooded an area west of King Street, Queen Street, Church Street and Greyfriars Road to London Road where the water rushed from the direction of the South Gates and rapidly became over 2ft in

Keeping their gals feet dry –
piggy backs in the flood
waters at King's Lynn.
(Sheila Flynn)

depth. Buses and cars succeeded for a brief spell to ford the waters but eventually vehicles became stranded and traffic was diverted through the back streets of the town via Tennyson and Vancouver Avenues. For a short time the water in London Road stopped near the entrance to the hospital but then rose again until it met the flood water pushing its way from the Millfleet. Fears were aroused as water poured into the Isolation hospital. A Sister climbed out of a window and waded through the deepening waters to London Road for help. Ambulance men carried the children out and they were taken to Thurlow House, (the nurse's training school) for safety. The waters then ran from London Road into Windsor Road to the statue at the junction of Guanock Terrace. In the town centre the angry river now swirled from the quaysides and along the narrow streets leading from them into the Saturday Market Place where parked cars were soon awash and the police station was virtually cut off to foot traffic

At about the same time waters surged over the bank near the Cut Bridge and washed over a very large area from the level crossing on Wisbech Road to the Cooper Ball Bearing Company, driving on as far as the South Lynn Railways Station, embracing the council housing estate, West Norfolk Farmers Manure Chemical Co. (the old "Muck Works") off Saddlebow Road, gas works and railway coal sidings up the river, it also backed up to flood an area behind the cemetery on Hardwick Road.

Pouring into the narrow South Lynn streets bitterly cold, filthy water crashed into Queen's Avenue and the Diamond Street area picking up cars and smashed them into fences. Brick walls and fences were torn down in the wake of the water which mercilessly pushed in unprotected doors and smashed through windows forcing water to flow through houses and blocked escape routes with furniture. Families hastily took refuge in upstairs rooms, in most cases without having time to even take up floor coverings or treasured property. Mrs Joan Mayne was living at the time at 21 Diamond Street with her husband (Who was at work at the "Muck Works" when the floods hit.), her mother and 4 year old daughter Helen. In an interview with the *Lynn News* Mrs Mayne recalled she had not heard any warnings, her first indication of the incoming water was after Helen had spilt some Lucozade; "I went to get a cloth to wipe it up when I saw the water coming in the door…We had sash windows and it was coming through the window frames before you could turn round. It was up to your waist in a few seconds." As the water filled the ground floor Mrs Mayne ushered her mother and daughter up the stairs to the bedrooms. Turning back to rescue Helen's cherished doll's house Christmas present, the torrent of water was such it was clearly too dangerous. Looking out of their upstairs windows Mrs Mayne remembers the area simply being surrounded by water. Later in the evening one of the many pigs kept on Harding's Pits allotments that had been drowned by the floods floated by her window. The many pigs drowned in the waters appeared all over the area having been swept along with the waters, one was found in an apple tree when the waters subsided, another was swept in through a broken sitting room window.

Rescue squads led by police and firemen were soon in action but their rescue attempts were greatly hampered as street lights failed or exploded in the waters, the electricity supply went down and bands of good willed neighbours got together armed only with torches to check on neighbours and call for help if necessary. At about 7.30pm the flood waters affected the telephone cables and fire service control was put out of order. Showing great initiative from knowing the Control centre lines were "out of area lines" based on King's Lynn's exchange and that local telephones were based on the Wooton exchange, the firewoman at the control centre thought it was worth a try stationing a retained fireman in a nearby telephone kiosk together with a messenger having asked the King's Lynn Telephone Exchange to divert the incoming calls to the kiosk number. Half and hour later even these lines failed so the innovative firewoman checked the nearby pub, found their phone still connected to the one surviving Wooton exchange line and took her log book and message pads across to the nearby Swan Inn and there set up the control using a leading fireman to carry any instructions to the local station. Experiencing similar problems the Lynn police set up control centre first in a nearby butchers shop and eventually ended up in a garage.

The local company of the Home Guard (one of the Home Guard units re-raised after their wartime stand-down for the Suez Crisis in 1952) were soon able to provide wireless communications between the temporary control and the fire station, a line later transferred to a field telephone provided by Cambridge Fire Brigade (summoned to assist the disaster in the town by a fire brigade alert at 7.49pm) thereby enabling an efficient wireless communication with the town.

The official Norfolk Fire Service County Control Report highlights the unfolding events of the flood disaster and other challenges thrown at them at Lynn:

"At 20.25 hours to add to the already heavy commitments, a fire call was received at both Gayton Road Fire Station, King's Lynn and Downham Market Fire Station to Shouldham Thorpe where stacks were on fire. This was followed a few minutes later by a further fire call to South Runcton station that stacks were involved. Appliances from King's Lynn, Downham Market and Massingham were sent. It eventually transpired that there was only one fire.

At 22.26 hours a further fire in the King's Lynn area requiring the attendance of two appliances was received from South Lynn Railway Station where a carbide store was involved. Owing to extensive flooding in King's Lynn a detour via Setch was ordered.

At 23.05 a fire call was received at King's Lynn due to the flood water affecting the electricity supply of a house. The effect of the water entering the electricity cables was further felt in King's Lynn and other fire calls were received.

At 23.30 King's Lynn reported that three trucks, three rubber dinghies and 27 airmen, one ambulance and two medical orderlies with a flight Sergeant in charge were in attendance from RAF Marham.

At 01.25 hours an urgent an urgent message was received at King's Lynn to pump out flood water from the Gas Works as the fires were in danger of being extinguished. This was followed at 02.22 hours with another most urgent request from the West Norfolk Farmers Manure & Chemical Co. to pump out flood water from their plant, which, if not done quickly, would produce a concentration of poisonous fumes.

The arrival of collapsible dinghies was reported by King's Lynn and ordered on at 03.04 hours to both Snettisham and Hunstanton beaches."

The worst of the flooding was over, the waters would begin to subside but now came the harrowing experience of discovering the extent of the damage inflicted by the surge and discovering those who had not survived. An information centre was set up at the Union Chapel on the Wisbech Road where a council official and a police officer checked names, kept a record of information about families in the district and answered queries from people concerned about relatives.

Voluntary organisation members were often presented with the agonising decision of protecting their home or reporting themselves for duty to their headquarters. Eighteen members of the King's Lynn St John Ambulance No.1 and 2 Divisions reported for duty on the night of the flood. Their work began with the establishment of a Rest Centre at their London Road Headquarters, St John Ambulance man Harry Ellis opened the hall and recalled "I soon had the old coke stove heating up and the kettle on for tea. Some people on Providence Street gave me tinned milk, tea, sugar, cakes and biscuits, which was quite something – it was rationed then! We had about fifty or sixty people through our hands that night, many with minor injuries." Other duties carried out by the St John volunteers included assisting the evacuation of victims, rendering emergency first aid and the removing the sick to hospital. The official report of King's Lynn St John Ambulance Division gives an idea of the sacrifice and dedication to service given by personnel during the flood emergency:

"Private H G Ellis was first man on duty. On Saturday, the night of the flood from 9pm till 4am next morning assisted police and hospital nurses in rescue work. Two serious first aid cases. Carried through 3ft of water an urgent maternity case from house to hospital...Did excellent work throughout, overtires his strength and had to rest for a day from his railway work. Divisional Superintendent A E Stringer was badly affected, his house flooded to the extent of 3ft. On Saturday evening when he was on his way to duty at a cinema he noticed the high tide and returned home in case he should be required as the tide had still 2 hours to go. Almost immediately at 6.15pm the manager of the Gas Works (where he was employed) sent for him to report at one to preserve the public supply as the water had got in. He was kept there until 5.30pm on the following day (Sunday). After spending a couple of hours at home trying to clean up the mess he contacted all available members instructing them to assist in the evacuation of victims. He carried on all day on St John work without food (his home having been destroyed) until 5.30pm when he had to find somewhere to sleep and live. From Monday to Friday he carried on with St John work in his spare time and then collapsed at the Gas Works and had to be taken home and ordered to bed.

Supt A W Croote and many of the members of King's Lynn No.2 Division lived in South Lynn where the worst of the floods hit and did not report in but rather went straight in and worked tirelessly with their neighbours to rescue and support other neighbours in need. "

A concerned Queen Elizabeth accompanied by the Duke of Edinburgh and the Duke of Gloucester (back to camera), with King's Lynn civic leaders viewing the flood damaged town on 2 February 1953 (*Norfolk Constabulary Archives*)

As the waters subsided the extent of the flooding soon became clear. About one fifth of the town's area had been under water, over 3000 houses had been affected by floods in Lynn alone. The depth of the waters varied from 4ft on London Road to 6ft 6 inches on the Wisbech Road. In some houses the water had almost reached the height of the front door, in others mantel shelf level while in some of the smaller houses in the South Lynn area water came near to ground floor ceilings. Once the waters abated householders were confronted with homes filled with thick mud, furniture tipped up, smashed or washed out of the house altogether broken glass and crockery everywhere.

Devastation was everywhere the water engulfed. In Lynn docks the water had derailed a locomotive and every warehouse, with the exception of the Princess Margaret warehouse, was flooded. The hydraulic pumping plants was flooded and the dock gates had to be closed manually. South Lynn Railway Station and Marshalling Yards were seriously affected, the flooding of the electricity sub-station caused the failure of the signalling system and no goods wagons could be moved. Electricity was restored piecemeal and with the largest coal dump in the town under water solid fuel was brought in by army lorries from Her Majesty the Queen's estate at Sandringham.

Four of the Lynn churches, namely: St Margarets, All Saints, St Nicholas and St Marys were flooded up to depths of two feet, pews, chairs, hassocks floated in the aisles and before the altars. Over 34 separate pumping incidents were carried out by the Lynn Fire Brigade which included such public buildings as the Guildhall, St James's Hospital, St James's Boys School and the Majestic Cinema as well as a wide selection of business premises.

On February 4th the inquest on the 15 Lynn flood victims was convened at the Town Hall before the Borough Coroner Mr G H C Stavely. It was soon clear from the testimony of Police Sergeant W. Shephard all the people who died when the deluge hit South Lynn were elderly and had no chance of survival because of the speed in which their homes were flooded. They jury were instructed that 14 of the victims were elderly; five aged over 80, eight over 70 and one over 60 were all found floating in the downstairs rooms of their homes and that they all had died from accidental drowning. The other, Alfred Robert Bailey,

MAP OF KING'S LYNN CENTRE SHOWING AREAS OF FLOODING IN 1953 AND KEY POINTS.

KEY TO PLAN :– ① TOWN HALL. ② NEW POLICE H.Q. ③ UNION CHAPEL ④ WEST LYNN POLICE BOX. ⑤ WELLESL ST. DRILL HALL. ⑥ CORPORATION DEPOT. ⑦ FIRE STATION. ⑧ AMBULANCE H.Q. ⑨ N.LYNN POL.BO ▨ FLOODED AREA 1953. ▨ WORST AFFECTED AREA 1953

THE BOROUGH OF KING'S LYNN

FLOOD ACTION BOOKLET

For the use of the Police, H.M. Forces, the Fire Service, the Ambulance Service, the Civil Defence Services, the Welfare Officer, the Welfare Services and the staff of the King's Lynn Borough Council.

Compiled by F. Calvert, Superintendent of Police, Norfolk Constabulary, King's Lynn.

The cost of printing this booklet has been borne by the King's Lynn Borough Council in a desire to ensure the co-ordination of all services.

The Borough of King's Lynn Flood Action Booklet and map of the flooded area in the town produced two months after the deluge.

a 67 year old retired policeman, had been discovered dry and away from the water on the stairs of his home on Queen's Avenue. He was found to have died of shock brought on by the deluge's sudden arrival at his house. Once the verdicts had been returned expressed sympathy to the relatives on behalf of the town, concluding, "This is a mournful day for the borough."

A complete list of the victims is as follows:

Mr Samuel and Mrs Louisa Chapman, aged 72 and 74 respectively were found at 18 Hockham Street along with their guest Miss Edith Constance Neave (61). In the same street, Mrs Hammond drowned at 17 and widow Mrs Annie Baxter at number 34. In Diamond Street, Mr Thomas Burrows (83) at 18 and Mrs Ethelinda Rix (79) of number 15. In Winfarthing Avenue, Mr George Lloyd (75) and Mrs Hannah Lloyd (75) of number 28. Widow, Mrs Elizabeth Vice (85) of 4 Ouse Avenue, widow Mrs Mary Cole (70) of 10 Langham Street, widow Mrs Eliza Lift (88) of 16 Portland Place, Mrs Elizabeth Dye (84) of 20 Wisbech Road and retired schoolmaster Mr Edgeley Richard Bunn (81) of 29 Queen's Avenue. The body of ex-PC Alfred Bailey (67) who died of coronary thrombosis, was found at 44 Queen's Avenue.

SNETTISHAM

In the histories and numerous articles that have been written about the East Coast Floods, the impact of the North Sea surge on the settlements at Snettisham has often been glossed over with just a brief few lines or has been shamefully omitted altogether. This little village lost 25 people, the second highest death toll of anywhere in Norfolk and Suffolk and it would have been far worse had it not been for the bravery, spirit and resourcefulness of local people working together to help their neighbours. A posthumous Albert Medal and four British Empire Medals were awarded to local people for gallantry here.

Snettisham is a village of two parts. It has its satellite beach settlement which consisted of self built bungalows some of which served as holiday dwellings, family homes and retirement residences. The bungalows stood cheek by jowl with a motley collection of beach huts, chalets, caravans, timber and asbestos shacks and a small holiday camp. Behind the shingle beach was a sand and gravel company's extraction works with a large lagoon which extended for quite some distance along the mile or so of road between the beach settlement and the attractively built main inland village of Snettisham.

Residents in the village with friends and family in Lynn were alerted to the approaching deluge by telephone from about 6.15pm. From bitter experience of flooding in 1949 Snettisham villagers realised such weather conditions were serious trouble and a few set out of their own accord along the mile or so of beach road to alert the beach residents. Half a mile into their journey, near the holiday camp, the water was found across the road and a crowd of people were already escaping the tide. These people and many others were taken by the limited transport to the Station Inn and sat by the fire to warm up and dry out.

Hazel Beckerton (right) and her mother, Vera, in front of their ruined bungalow at Snettisham (*East Midland Allied Press Ltd*)

The journeys between the beach and the pub became numerous and more and more people were recovered by the village volunteers. It was not long before the old inn became like a makeshift advanced dressing station as those trained in medical skills and first aid ministered to the sick and injured with household medical kits. Other rescued people were taken to the Church Hall and later to Leslie's Tea Rooms where they were given cups of tea. As the long night wore on village rescue parties experienced the horror of having those held in their arms swept away from their grasp, within yards of safety, by the end of the night the Church Rooms became a temporary morgue.

The first call for assistance was made to Heacham Fire Station at 19.00 hours when an appliance was sent and the District Fire Officer followed in his car. The District Fire Officer foundered at the same half-mile point in the road where the villagers had been blocked by the water. Assuming the Heacham fire engine had made it to the beach the officer and the local policeman he encountered on the way surveyed the scene. The current of the water, fast moving debris and the force of the gale (estimated at 60mph) left them no option but to turn back and seek further assistance.

It was also about this time Police Sergeant Gerald Bunney of Dersingham tried to gain access to Snettisham Beach along the agricultural road at Dersingham and was within a mile of the sea when he saw torrential flood water rushing inland. He turned and raced the floods back to Dersingham to warn the local inhabitants. He then went to Snettisham where he took charge of the rescue operations. He organised a rescue party and at the head of a rope lifeline penetrated into the surging flood waters which, at times, came up to the necks of the rescuers. The current was so strong that only very slow progress could be made and after three quarters of a mile the rescue team split up. Sgt Bunney led a party to a house which was flooded to the first floor and rescued 18 persons. During this rescue one of the rescuers, who was carrying a child, was attacked with cramp and fell in the water. Sgt Bunney immediately helped him and both the man and child were brought to dry land thanks to the brave Sergeant. Helping throughout the next day he worked till totally exhausted he had to retire to his home. In the Flood Honours list of April 1953 Sgt Bunney was awarded the BEM for his gallantry.

On the beach itself was the bungalow home of Frederick and Vera Beckerton where they lived with their children; Peter, Michael, John and Hazel. It had been a day of excitement for the household as their first television set had arrived that very morning and two of the children's friends; Shirley Baxter and Michael Bryan (London foster-children who lived with Mr and Mrs Walton in a bungalow a few yards away.) had joined them to enjoy the Saturday tea-time programmes. It was just as the children's programme ended the Beckerton's eldest son, Peter, came in and reported the sea was coming over the bank.

Accompanied by his father, Peter set off on a journey of a few hundred yards to the Walton's house to bring the couple, both in their sixties, (Mr Walton was an invalid) and their third foster child back to the Beckerton home to weather the storm together. Outside Peter and his father soon found the situation had become far worse than they had imagined but they pushed on. With sea water rising to their waists Peter told his father to go back. Taking a last look back while battling his return home against the watery swell Mr Beckerton saw his son reach the Walton's door. It could have only been seconds after that the surge swept Peter and the Walton's bungalow away.

Returning home Frederick Beckerton found to his horror the sea had already breached the veranda doors. Trying to jam the doors closed the effort against the sea onslaught was pointless. The Beckerton family retreated to the kitchen. Mrs Beckerton lined the children

Nineteen-year old Snettisham floods hero Peter Beckerton (*Hazel Bolton*)

Mrs Vera Beckerton BEM, with the five children she rescued. Standing next to her mum is daughter Hazel and from left to right along the front are Michael Beckerton (9), Shirley Baxter (11), John Beckerton (7) and Michael Bryan (*East Midland Allied Press Ltd*).

up against the door to keep it open, realising if it closed it would be held fast by water and their only escape route closed. Snatching sheets from the linen cupboard Mrs Beckerton went outside and lashed their old ten-foot lugsail boat fast. With water chest high the Beckertons helped the children into the boat one by one. This was to prove to be only the beginning of a seven-hour ordeal. While the children bailed out the boat with cake tins the Beckerton parents stood up to their necks in water to keep the boat afloat in the poor shelter afforded by the battered bungalow. Timber and broken bits of furniture from other wrecked houses hammered into them as it swept past on the surge – they even saw a complete bungalow sail past.

With the hour well past midnight the waters receded presenting a new danger where the Beckertons could be drawn out to sea. However their initial fears were soon allayed as the sea level rapidly dropped and they found themselves on a shingle bank. Finding a water logged trunk with blankets inside nearby they wrapped each of the children in the wet coverings – it was better than nothing. Having lost all track of time their decision was what to do next – a decision which needed to be made quickly before the inevitable return of the next tide.

At the same time and having already had a hell of a night village policeman PC Henry Ernest Nobbs had mustered help and was making his way back up the beach road. He had already helped organise a rope line rescues with Sgt Bunney and had gone into the flood waters to rescue a man who was clinging to a telegraph pole. Tieing the rope from telegraph pole to telegraph pole and leaving a life line back to safety he grabbed the exhausted man and returned him to safety. Making good ground over the receding waters PC Nobbs employed the rope tactic to cross the lake in the pits behind the shingle bank. PC Nobbs found the Beckertons and their young charges. Eleven more survivors were recovered from the shingle bank and wrecked houses by the gallant Constable, with the help of his village volunteer rescue party. For their bravery on that fateful night both PC Nobbs and Mrs Beckerton were both awarded the British Empire Medal. Her son's body had only been discovered washed up a few weeks before, his efforts to rescue the Walton's and their foster child had been in vain as they too had been found drowned. Mrs Beckerton took no delight in her award until the news arrived of the posthumous award of the Albert Medal to her beloved son for his gallantry on that terrible night – gallantry for which this brave young man gave the ultimate sacrifice but an award which was a constant source of solace and pride for the rest of his mother's life.

Snettisham resident Mr H W Temple-Cole summed up to the courageous of the village "The real heroes of the night were undoubtedly just ordinary people-the village copper, the plumber, the electrician, three of four farmers or sons of farmers, a couple of Red Cross men (later) and one or two firemen. They all did a jolly fine job under conditions which, up till then, I would have been certain that it would be impossible to stand."

Hazel Bolton pauses for a moment after laying flowers on her hero brother's grave at Snettisham, 2002.

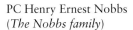

PC Henry Ernest Nobbs (*The Nobbs family*)

Bungalows wrecked by the floods at Snettisham (*David Bocking*)

A truck remains slumped in the ditch where the flood waters pushed it at Snettisham.

The morning sunlight and abating waters revealed an horrific scene of devastation. The abandoned Heacham Fire engine had not reached the beach, it stood forlorn and battered on the coast road its crew having scrambled for their lives onto the roof when the engine failed in the water. The crew had afterwards managed to wade to safety but went into the maelstrom again to give valuable assistance in the rescue bids. The official fire brigade reports' simplicity reflects the futility of attempting to find words adequate to describe the morning after the storm

"The following day with the police the area was searched for persons that might be alive and to recover bodies. The force of the sea and wind had swept cars and vans from the road and a large section of the sea groyne had been carried half a mile inland across the road. The devastation at Snettisham beach was immense."

Mr David Bocking, a lifelong resident of Snettisham, who was involved with rescues throughout that fateful night recalled the devastation revealed by the abating waters and the morning light. He recalls the debris of peoples' homes and their effects strewn all over the area and caught on fences. The worst part of all was recovering the bodies of those who had perished.

"I was dreading going on the beach. I was brought up there so knew everybody. I remember getting our neighbour and his wife out with rope lines on the night. About half an hour after he was rescued the neighbour had returned saying "I've come back for my money." I found him in the dyke on the Wednesday. My father and I searched the area over the following days for bodies of animals and people. We were getting a sow out with a rope round it when father said "I've got one over here." It turned out to be a human body and in that afternoon we found three in a very short space of time. One lady was hanging upside down in bushes. They'd driven along the road in their car and the tide had swished them round and washed them both out the back doors which were flung wide open.

Another friend, his mother has swum the English Channel a couple of times and it was too much for her, she drowned. We were looking for her son for a matter of weeks. When the water cleared from them big pits near the beach we found him stood upright in the water. The shingle had got into his welly boots and when they found him he looked as though he was still alive. Often I've laid in bed and woke up in a sweat as everything comes back to me."

Over the ensuing weeks inquests were held at Snettisham and Dersingham where some of the bodies were washed up. On 4 February Mr L H Allwood the Dereham and District Coroner opened an inquest to examine six of the dead at Snettisham. Among the dead were Mrs Evelyn Frances Mortimer (27) and her sons John (4) and Roger (1) the wife and two children of Mr Mortimer, a Birmingham dentist who was a locum tenens in the village and the only survivor of his family exposed to the flood at their home on the South Beach. Other victims of the flood discussed at the inquest were Mrs Eileen O'Brien (39) of *Inglenook*, Beach Road, Albert Bairdstone (14) of 77 The Beach, and Mr Edward John Sandy of *The Cedars* also on Beach Road. Death from accidental drowning was the verdict in every case.

HEACHAM

About 6.30pm the North Sea surge hit Heacham South Beach tearing through the massive concrete sea wall and smashed the parapet of the North Beach creating a gaping 300yd breach. Rather like at Snettisham, there were over a hundred of holiday bungalows, set back and along its beach, a number of which had become year round residences. Over 100 of these homes were simply swept away here leaving only three bungalows intact amongst the debris after the storm. When the flood hit Heacham the local fire engine was attending the emergency at Snettisham and, as it transpired, would not return that night. The Fire Brigade official report picks up the story:

"The call to Heacham Beach (Where two persons were reported trapped in a bungalow) was not received until 19.50 hours, some hour and a half after the flooding started. The second appliance from Heacham responded but after finding the water was toop deep to proceed further than the Railway Station the crew waded to the bungalow where two persons were found. In a farmhouse and a bungalow both showing lights the occupiers were found comparatively safe. The water was three to four feet deep and the current so strong that if the men had left a protecting bank they would have been swept away. A quarter of a mile nearer the sea, where 5 lives were lost, it was impossible to reach the spot even by boat due to the exceptionally strong current and the heavy debris and wreckage in the water."

Village folks banded together to help each other and aid rescue bids but because of the suddenness and ferocity of the sea surge 9 residents perished. Among them an affectionately remembered elderly local man named Ernie Wright. Thought to have been swept away by the flood waters his body was not recovered by searchers. He was, however, found some time later in the roof space of his home, completely dry but tragically dead from the shock he suffered escaping the floods.

HUNSTANTON

Hunstanton received the brunt of the sea's assault upon Norfolk. Despite numerous acts of gallantry, many of which were later officially recognised in the flood gallantry awards the rapidity and power of the North Sea surge against the wooden coastal bungalows near Hunstanton (many of which were occupied by American servicemen and their families) saw the highest death toll of anywhere in the county with 31 dead. Taking into account the deaths at nearby Snettisham and Heacham this area of coastline suffered more loss of life than anywhere else in Eastern England during the 1953 flood disaster, its nearest rivals being Canvey Island (Essex) with 58 dead, Felixtowe, where 40 people died when a seaside prefab estate was swept away and Jaywick (Essex) where 37 drowned when a housing estate was engulfed by the flooding sea waters. The Norfolk County planning officer recorded simply " The most terrible scene of the disaster was south of Hunstanton."

At about 7.00pm an estimated 7ft tall wall of water smashed through the beach bungalow community near Hunstanton. These bungalows, of predominantly wooden construction, although never intended for permanent occupation were occupied by many US servicemen and their young families; people living here stood little or no chance of survival when the waters hit. The Fire Brigade report explains:

"The area of Hunstanton affected is bordered on the north by the railway station, on the east by the railway line and mainly comprised an area of summer residences and an amusement park. The sea came over the wall in this area and battered the houses which

South Beach Road, Hunstanton pictured as the floods began to abate revealing the dangerous debris that had been concealed under the water. The sunken Weasel in the foreground is the one that had been carrying Ambulanceman Les Framingham, Police Sergeant Harry Spencer and Neil Quincey.

Staff Sergeant Freeman A. Kilpatrick USAAF being decorated with the George Medal for his gallantry during the floods at Hunstanton. (*Steve Snelling*)

are at a low level. Sand was washed up to a considerable height in some parts while in others the land was scoured to a very dangerous depth particularly along the track of the sewage outfall. In a very short time of the sea coming over the wall it was impossible to get into the area."

As the water poured between the north end of Hunstanton South Beach wall and the southern end of the North Parade through the so-called "Hunstanton Gap" (an area long recognised as a glaring defect along this section of coastal defences) one of the first to realise the magnitude of the flood peril as it hit Hunstanton was Staff Sergeant Freeman A Kilpatrick. Serving in the 3rd Communications Squadron at Sculthorpe he was at home in his South Beach bungalow with his wife and child when the first waters flooded the community. Having moved his own family into relative safety in the upper space of his home he thought of his neighbours. In the words of his citation "without regard for his own safety, ventured out into the storm for the purpose of warning other families, both American and English, of the impending disaster." Swimming through raging water Kilpatrick succeeded in rescuing no fewer than 18 people at great risk to his own life. This done he then "swam back to his home to evacuate his wife, child and two English people to the roof of his home, where they remained until the following morning when rescued." For his gallantry Freeman A. Kilpatrick was awarded the George Medal.

The official fire brigade report continues:

"At 19.16 hours a call was received at Hunstanton Fire Station from South Beach Road where persons were reported trapped, and an appliance with the officer in charge of the station attended. When the appliance arrived at the waters edge it was found that no rescue work could be performed except by means of boats. A DUKW owned by a local person had been participating in rescue work but had overturned. Our officer with a civilian obtained a rowing boat and endeavoured to search the area for persons that were still trapped. Conditions were deplorable due to high wind, sleet, flooding and sea which broke over the boat continuously. Persons were located in a house but in endeavouring to negotiate the boat the current was so strong that the rowlocks of the boat were broken and it drifted past the house. The boat was tied up to the remains of another house to save being swept away. By this time the USA air sea rescue craft were available and a rescue boat which was out of commission drifted by. Our officer in the rowing boat was able to release an obstruction fouling the propellor of this boat but on release it was found that the rudder of the rescue craft was smashed. Our officer took over as coxswain of a second craft which was in need of somebody with local knowledge and a number of people were picked up."

The gaunt shell of the home of Mrs. Coates on South Beach Road, Hunstanton.

A scene of utter destruction on South Beach Road, Hunstanton. Many folks had little chance of survival when the wall of water hit their homes.

Below left: More wrecked houses and the tragic remnants of homes stewn around South Beach Road, Hunstanton.

Below right: The wrecked bungalow '*Jocadoma*' still surrounded by water on South Beach Road, Hunstanton.

At 7.27pm the train for Lynn left Hunstanton. Five hundred yards out of the station it hit water, at about three quarters of a mile down the line, just past the spinney, when a wooden bungalow floated from its foundations drifted in front of the steam engine and stopped it dead. Railwayman Tony Framingham had (unofficially) caught the train rather than attempt to cycle home to Heacham and recalled his night of the floods for the *Lynn News*:

"The engine's pipes burst on the front and the engine came to a horrible juddering stand. The water rose very rapidly right up to the top of the seats. There was only one carriage on the train and I was travelling in the Guard's van...I went through to the passengers. There was a family, the Hastings, with their two children, I picked up the children and put them in the luggage rack. The guardsman was Walter Bruce, the driver Frank Parnell and the fireman was Dougie Skate.

We could see bungalows were piling in behind us, we couldn't run the train back because the pipes were broken. The driver and the fireman clambered over the tender and got in through the carriage door. Dougie Skate went back over the tender to have a look in the firebox and to see what he could do about the engine. He made his way around the front and he filled the steam pipes with old oily rags and then came back to us. He then said he would try and see if we could get steam up and make it back through the water. We broke up a cabinet in the guards van for tinder and he put it with some clinker that was left in the top of the firebox...We didn't really have enough pressure up but he knew in his own mind that once he managed to get it to move he would never stop. He got it to move and we backed up about half way to the station. When the engine got back to the station I looked at it covered in red rust, reeds and rushes and I thought 'you beauty.' Without a doubt Dougie Skate was a hero that night". Mr Framingham adds as a footnote to his story that the bungalow drifting in front of the train was found to be a blessing in disguise: "When the waters abated we saw that if the train hadn't been blocked it would have travelled the hundred yards or so down the line to where the tracks had been ripped up by the tide and we would all have been done for!"

Hunstanton St John Ambulance Divisional Superintendent R W Smith takes up the story of how the town was made aware and reacted to the flood in his confidential report written by hand from his sick bed while recovering from the effects of exposure during flood rescues:

"The first indication we had of anything happening was "The Siren"! (At about 7.00pm) Followed by another half hour later, we concluded it was a fire getting out of control, but within a few minutes the phone went – could I turn out at once and get all help, position a most disastrous affair had arisen, all bungalows etc. were marooned on South Beach, the sea wall had broken, high tide was pouring in.

A First Aid Post and Rest Centre was set up in the Sandringham Hotel Ballroom. I was first on the scene here (about 8.00pm) where a dance was in progress. They knew nothing of what had happened – the MC approached me in amazement when he saw me with haversack, stretcher and blankets. Money was repaid to the dancers but I must say the American dancers immediately came up to me and offered to stay if I wished. I thanked them, several stayed on duty with me for 12 hours – without a break, were of immense help to me and others. The WVS soon found us and everything was soon ready to receive casualties, the first of many arriving at about 10pm."

By 8.00pm news of the disaster had reached RAF Sculthorpe and the base group captain, Colonel Sibenaler sent out for volunteers to assist in rescue work. Airman 3rd Class Reis Leming recalled:

"We came along directly with rescue equipment including the aluminium boats used for sea rescues but those were no use in the strong wind, and besides the propellers got tangled up in the wires. "I suppose it was about 8.45 that we launched the first of these and I know I had been in and out of the icy water many times until about midnight when I went up to the headquarters at the Sandringham Hotel to change my clothes. When I got back near the end of South beach I put on my exposure suit (waterproof yellow rubber suit) and decided to push a rubber dinghy.

Boy, it took some keeping into the wind and sometimes I was right under the water

Hunstanton's tall young hero, Airman 3rd Class Reis Leming USAAF.

in the ditches. There was no-one else as tall as me – I am 6ft 3inches – so they couldn't help. Once the wind and a wave carried me and the dinghy right on top of a caravan but gradually I managed to get near the ruins of the bungalows and get people into the dinghy. Shucks, it wasn't much."

Reis's great modesty prevents a full account of his gallantry. We are however lucky to have been left a contemporary account of Airman Leming's action by Captain J M Viehman of 67 Squadron. Viehman stated that Leming had "travelled the entire length of the Hunstanton sea-front bungalows, a distance of about 3 quarters of a mile, returning each time to take people off the roofs of the crushed bungalows where there was enough debris to recognise and knocked and called for people." All the time the gale was howling around Reis as he fought against the current in constant danger from the floating debris, it was a miracle it missed him. His job was not made any easier as the bodies of the drowned floated by him. "At 4.45am Leming himself became unconscious and was taken to the hospital." Reis Leming was to become the first American recipient of The George Medal for his gallantry on that fatal night.

Reis had been treated by Divisional Superintendent Smith, whose account mentions an incident "at the sharp end:"

"Framingham had a very nasty experience and what one might say a very close "go." He had joined other helpers in a Weasel (a land and water rescue vehicle) but this soon became caught in wreckage, sunk and they were stranded. They eventually get to a two storey bungalow, managed to scramble in where others had already assembled. The position was getting serious, the raging sea under them was wrecking the house, and the floor began to sag all ropes. Children were rescued by the man I am treating in the photo [Smith had included a cutting and snapshot showing him treating Reis] Framingham and other men knew they would have to make a bold bid for it or be washed away, and this they did, waded through the floods nearly up to their necks. Despite his experience Framingham reported to the post but was soon sent home. I am pleased to report he is no worse for his experience."

Taxi driver Neil Quincey was also part of the rescue team trying to reach his wife Betty and their children from their South Beach home, he recalls his first-hand experiences of that fateful night:

"I was up at Sculthorpe that day and I was busy because it was pay day. It was a rough old day, about normal for that time of year. I had made trips to Lynn and Norwich but it was about half past six, quarter to seven time I got a trip back to Hunstanton. When I got there I was told there had been a call from home, so I went to the telephone exchange where the operator, Des Asker was talking to my wife Betty. The line never did get pulled down by the water. Betty told me the water had come over so I told Des to keep talking to her and I set off.

Some of the wrecked houses on South Beach Road from which Reis Leming pulled a number of people through flood waters to safety using a rubber dinghy.

When I got to the Eastern Counties bus garage on Southend Road the Americans were just beginning to arrive. The time must have been after 8pm and the water was already over the railway lines. There was a Weasel there and the captain only wanted American personnel on but I managed to get on with St John Ambulance man Les Framingham and Police Sergeant Harry Spencer.

I was shouting directions to the driver over the howling wind. I knew there was a concrete pillbox at the end of the road which we had to avoid so I told the driver to head towards the sea. For some reason he seemed to keep wanting to turn left but if he'd done that we would have been swept into the bungalows. There was only a small light on the front of the boat and all you could see was the spray from the sea. I kept him going until we could see the silhouette of my bungalow and then he turned as quickly as he could and we were blown towards it.

As we came up to the bungalow the Weasel was still moving so Sgt Spencer and I jumped and caught hold of the balcony. I think the Americans thought they were going to wait outside like a taxi and the driver cut the engine. It rocked twice and engulfed by water it sunk. The next thing we knew we were hanging of the balcony and scrambling up. How at least one of us didn't drown it don't know.

We had arrived but we had lost the boat and everything else. We worried about what would happen at the next high tide which would come at about 7.30am so we kept dipping the water outside with a boathook to see how deep it was. We even had the idea of

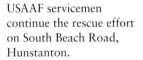

USAAF servicemen continue the rescue effort on South Beach Road, Hunstanton.

disconnecting the bath and floating the children out in it as soon as the tide went down a bit but then, it must have been about 4.00am we looked across to the bank opposite, near the fairground and saw lights and torches and a dinghy coming towards us. [The official report also praises Mr Quincey and Sgt Spencer for maintaining the only tele-communications over the one surviving phone line until they were rescued.] I now know the tall American pulling the dinghy was Reis Leming. I think he must have got the job because he was the tallest one among them. By the time he came across, the water had gone down to about 5ft. I put my son Bill (ten months) inside my jacket and got into the dinghy. Someone else took our other two daughters Susan (seven) and Jane (three). Sgt Spencer and Les Framingham jumped into the water and helped push the dinghy to safety. Many people like them risked their lives that night without a thought for themselves."

Divisional Superintendent Smith concludes his report with some personal observations of that fateful night:

" I must say how sad a picture it was as these poor rescued people in early hours of Sunday morning were brought in to the Sandringham and each told their story. One lad told me that his mother and father were washed away, another man told me his wife and

Amusement Park — "The morning after," Hunstanton No. 6.

child were in a bungalow which suddenly disappeared. An American suddenly broke down (and speaking in dazed stilted words) said "Wife and children gone. The house is not there." My saddest night was Sunday when I looked in at the temporary mortuary and saw a sweet little American boy, about the age of four, all dressed so warmly, beside a woman, no doubt his mother."

Divisional Superintendent Smith was awarded the British Empire Medal for his initiative and dedication during the floods, his recommendation for the award, endorsed by a letter of praise the Norfolk's Chief Constable, concludes:

"Under the direction of Mr Smith, there was a joint staff of American and British attending the patients. Mr. Smith, who is not a young man, was on continuous duty for 12 hours and the magnitude of his task and those who helped him can be gauged by the fact that 28 persons [the final death toll at Hunstanton was 31] were drowned. I am advised that Mr Smith, as First Aid leader in the town, took the initiative and it is largely due to

The wreckage of the Hunstanton amusement park still being buffeted by the waves on the morning after the flood.

The smashed concrete and bricks of the palisade and open air bathing pool, Hunstanton.

No. 4   Breach in Defences—South Beach, Hunstanton

The fatal breach in the sea defences at the South Beach, Hunstanton.

his action and thanks to the co-operation of the Americans, that the emergency arrangements, in such difficult circumstances, worked so smoothly."

As dawn broke and the waters abated the full horror of the damage caused by the wall of water was revealed. Of the hundreds of bungalows that stood between Heacham and Hunstanton beaches only three remained standing. On top of this scene of devastation and if the rescue workers didn't have enough to contend with the fresh water supply, washed over by the surging sea, failed by late morning. The Fire Brigade were asked if they could help but could not attempt such an undertaking on their now limited resources so they approached the local military at Britannia Barracks. Sadly they could not help directly in this case as they had no water trucks but suggested they contact Colchester Garrison who immediately despatched three lorries with water tanks of various sizes. Eleven water tenders, including one from Cambridgeshire Fire Brigade were ordered to Hunstanton for the purpose of filling tanks and for house to house water delivery. By night fall an adequate fresh water supply was available to the town, a service maintained until the piped fresh water supply was re-established to residents on 7 February.

The Queen and the Duke of Edinburgh put a brave face on the situation while viewing the flood damage at Hunstanton on 3 February 1953

With the coming of the dawn came the final harrowing realisation of the true death toll at Hunstanton. Bodies were recovered from houses and washed up on the beaches in the locality for weeks afterwards. One who witnessed the full horror of what had happened was the ex-Japanese prisoner of war headmaster of Hunstanton Primary School, Mr. George James. He especially recalled one of the most popular children in the school, 14 year-old Derek Stubbins. On Friday 30 January he had returned home with the proud news that he had been elected school captain. A conscientious boy, on the Saturday he had refused an invitation from friend to stay for tea because he didn't want to worry his parents by staying out later than anticipated. Derek arrived home an hour before the waters smashed through the defences. He died with his entire family in the deluge. Mr. James attended many funerals over the following weeks, the memories never left him.

Another tragic tale is that of 13 year-old Janet Papworth, a St John Ambulance cadet with Hunstanton Division. On the afternoon of 31 January she bid farewell to her family and walked out of her South Beach Road home and up into the town to attend a birthday party of fellow St John cadet, Shirley Turner. The flood prevented Janet's return home that fateful evening. On the following day Janet's mongrel dog, Trixie, found its way to the Turner's house shivering with cold and suffering from two broken ribs. Janet had no idea anything had happened to her family, at worst she thought they had been evacuated to a rest centre. The reality was heartbreaking: the surging waters had killed her mother and three sisters, Pat (15), Jennifer (11) and Susan (8) leaving Janet an orphan.

The complete roll of all thirty-one people killed at Hunstanton is as follows:

Fredrich Axford

Mabel Axford

Kathleen Coates

William Driver

Florence Driver

Samuel Hurling

Dorothy Hurling

Phyllis Papworth

Patricia Papworth

Jennifer Papworth

Susan Papworth

Ethel Southwell

William Stubbins

Derek Stubbins

Marjorie Stubbins

US Servicemen and their families
  killed while resident in Hunstanton

Bernard F. Bailey

Agnes L. Bailey

Pamela D. Bailey

Herbert E. Branch

Gladys M. Branch

Herbert E. Branch Jr.

Sandra K. Branch

Maynard W. Martin

Dorothy V. Martin

Russell O. Martin

Dorothy Martin

Russell O. Martin Jr.

John W. Martin

Rose E. Richardson

Joseph N. Richardson

James N. Richardson

The memorial to the victims of the 1953 floods at Hunstanton.

WELLS

The pleasant sea-side town of Wells was no stranger to flooding. Over the years local people had got used to listening out for coastguard warnings and maintained stocks of sandbags to plug up doorways and cellar gratings against encroaching waters. The large expanses of marsh and water inlets around Wells and across the Holkham Meals were directly in line for the first intimation of a surge moving southwards down the North Sea. One of the first to notice the threat on 31 January 1953 was Mr George Jay who was up Wells beach bait digging:

"I suppose that would be about one o'clock time in the afternoon. The tide was out then and we rowed across and we weren't far away and the wind was sou'west. About three o'clock that come out of the North, through onto the land and I turned around to our uncle Percy and said "That look to me as though our boat is afloat," "What," he said "it can't be. That can't ha' gout out that quick!" But I went and had a look and it was. The tide was well up and was about two and a half hours early." Beating a hasty retreat Mr Jay and his uncle got home safely packing their bait up and sent it off to their buyer on the train. By the time he returned to his home on Dogger Lane the water was already at least knee deep on Freeman Street. By the time the next train arrived the station was under 12ft of water. The water rushed through the van and carriages so quickly the guard of this train had to be transferred to dry land by rowing boat. The waters rushed in so quickly Mr R. Tuck, the signalman ended up being marooned in his signal box – an island amongst the waters – until the Sunday morning!

The tide had flowed over the quay wall at 5.00pm, by about 6.30pm the waters had risen higher than any other recorded floods in the town and breached the sea defences of Wells in four places. The embankment to the east of the town was breached near its western end and the sea flooded across Slade Marsh to the pond near North Hall Farm, Warham.

Aerial view of the flooded railway station at Wells-next-the-Sea.

This breach also saw waters surge across Church Marsh up to the foot of two furlong hill. The old Osterich Inn on Burnt Street had water in the ground floor rooms while on Polka Road only the glass globes on the top of the petrol pumps at the garage south of the railway station were visible above the flood water. In Staithe Street the water rose until it entered the back yard of the Golden Fleece Inn.

The embankment from the quay to the Point was breached in three places and the whole of the Holkham Marshes and part of Holkham Park were flooded. One breach was close to the northern end, where the old ship's channel left Wells channel for Holkham Staithe and Abraham's Bosom. The torrent through this carried away the Jubilee Café. A second breach occurred about half way along the embankment. The torrent there scoured out a hole in the marshland about 15ft deep and an acre in area. The third breach occurred near the quay, just north of the old lifeboat house.

Despite the wind many folks had ventured out on that fateful Saturday night. The fish and chip shops of the town were doing brisk business and locals huddled a little closer together in the queues bathed in the warm amber light of the shops. A good house was attending the Regal Cinema where the Technicolour features of "Lassie" in *The Painted Hills* and *Across the Wide Missouri* starring Clark Gable were showing. Amongst the audience was Mr Leslie Eaton who had taken his young son Howard to the performance. The following is an account compiled from his gallantry citation, police reports and an official letter of thanks from Wells Town Council.

The film came to an abrupt end when at 5.15pm a flood alert notice was flashed on the screen. Mr Eaton was not only the local Gas Works manager but the Superintendent of the local St John Ambulance Division – he knew the town and he knew the people who would need his help. Ensuring his little boy was escorted home safely Leslie ran to the St John Headquarters near the church, grabbed a stretcher and first aid equipment and instantly made for the home of Mrs Herbert Kemp of Quayside. He knew this lady to be bedridden with arthritis. By the time he arrived Mrs Kemp had been removed from her bed and had been laid on a table floating in about 4 or 5ft of water in the room. Mr Eaton, being 6ft 2" high, but shoulder deep, was able to carry Mrs Kemp to the stretcher and assisted by PC Sizeland, lifted her to safety. "But for Supt Eaton's forethought and the taking of instant action, coupled to personal risk, Mrs Kemp would have been drowned."

Below left: The 160 ton Sea Cadet training MTB Terra Nova is left stranded after being floated on to the dockside by the risen waters at Wells during the night of 31 January 1953. (Gressenhall Farm and Workhouse Museum of Norfolk Life)

Below right: The backs of damaged houses washed out by flood waters on Freeman Street viewed from the Recreation Ground, pictured on 1 February 1953 (Gressenhall Farm and Workhouse Museum of Norfolk Life)

Mr Eaton then led a house to house search of properties on the seaward side of Freeman Street, the Recreation Ground side of which had been washed away by surging flood. As he went from building to building Leslie, remembered his duty to community safety as Manager of the Gas Works and ensured all the gas was turned off in the properties to avoid dangers of explosion. At the conclusion of a general check amid the ruins, it was found that a middle-aged brother and sister – Mr S and Miss L Dickerson were missing.

In the teeth of the gale, flood and darkness, Supt Eaton entered the ruined side of the

Freeman Street, Wells on the morning after the flood. (*Bygones Collection, Holkham*)

Wells St John Ambulance Superintendents, husband and wife Leslie and Barbara Eaton looking at Leslie's award for gallantry in the floods at Wells. Leslie received the St John Ambulance Life Saving Medal (Silver Class); in his recommendation for the award County Commissioner Sir Thomas Cook described him as '...bravest of the lot.' (*the late Leslie Eaton*)

house but found nobody. He then remembered that the two houses had been knocked into one and the only means of entry to a certain room, due to water, was through the first floor window. There he found the Dickersons crouching and dazed. He then carried each of them to safety. Supt Eaton's citation concludes "Throughout the immediate danger, flood and consequent house collapse, involving rescues at great personal risk and subsequent to the water receding the conduct of Supt Eaton as an example and inspiration to others, has been outstanding." This was the first but not the last act of gallantry in the town of Wells that night.

In the area of one of the first breaches at Holkham, Police Sergeant N. Hewitt of Wells, with the Wells lifeboat coxswain Mr W R Cox and four members of the lifeboat crew launched a 15ft boat outside the entrance of Holkham Victoria Hotel and rowed across the marshes to the house one and a half miles away. They first rescued a sick man named Mr Murton then rowed out again for Mr Murton's wife, daughter in law and their child. This

The floods viewed from the Holkham Estate driveway looking across the coast road with Lady Ann's Drive to the right. (*Bygones Collection, Holkham*)

The Wells to Heacham railway line submerged by flood waters.

journey had been a treacherous one as on these marshes many cattle had been trapped by flood – to have struck one of these would have meant almost certain disaster.

The Coastguard Station Officer J Scott was on duty at the beach lookout at Wells, incredibly the waters had breached the coast here in such a way it was only when he went off duty at 8pm that he found he was cut off by the floods! He risked a walk to the beach to the lifeboat house and with the aid of his bicycle lamp flashed morse signals with the hope of attracting the attention of somebody on the quay. He failed to get any reply and decided to return to the lookout and await daylight. The position, however, deteriorated and as waters approached the lookout Mr Scott made one last desperate attempt to summon help by signalling from the lifeboat house again at midnight. This time his signals were seen by Police Sergeant Hewitt who contacted the coastguard and a reply was flashed back "OK Coming."

Coastguard R Crown, his son Mr E. Crown, Harbourmaster Frank Smith and George Jay volunteered to make the trip. At 12.45am they embarked on their hazardous journey. Mr Jay takes up the story:

"We managed to drag a small boat over the top of the bank, got some oars and rowlocks and set off rowing down Beach Road. Course, we were going down the road and the water was up near telegraph wires. Well, we knew the first bank was there so we rowed round it the best we could. The water was rushing through into the harbour. In other words it was going east to west, going back into the harbour. We kept rowing down beach road when all of a sudden we came to another bank we didn't know was there. Well, it just picked the book up like a cork and we went over the bank at about 15 knots – in a row boat! We couldn't do anything about it. It swept us over on the mud banks.

Well, we managed to get out of the boat on what we call Bug's Bank but I had to get in again right smart because the sand was all alive and I went straight down to the top of my boots. Anyway, we got back in and carried on rowing down to the beach and we landed near the old lifeboat house (at about 3am). We then set off to find the coastguard. We found him and decided to row him back as far as the bridge...On the return journey we found we couldn't row, you could never have rowed against that, the way that was setting out there. We had to get our boat alongside the bank and walk her up, one of us in the boat holding her off with oars...It was pitch black all the while, we had a torch and that was all. You couldn't see nothing really. We knew by that time that the two breaches were there and we give them a wide berth. I know its easy enough to sit here and say it, but it's really true, we are lucky to be alive because there was all posts sticking up everywhere in that gap. We must have gone right between them or over the top."

The rescues of this gallant little crew didn't end there. On their return they assisted in the rescue attempts in the town and on the following day took the little boat out again to get Mr Tuck out of his signal box at the station.

Lady Cook (second from right), St John Ambulance personnel and a few locals around the flood relief van at Wells.

Thanks to the gallantry and public spirit of local people there were no flood fatalities at Wells. The water had reached depths of 15ft in areas like Beach Road and many families in the west of the town had been rendered homeless. Willing members of the public, voluntary workers of the St John Ambulance and Red Cross joined with the Police, Coast Guard and members of the Urban District Council working together to evacuate the unfortunate families. Many of these rescuers worked over a 12 hour period in terrible conditions often wading waist high in water to help others. Those rendered homeless were accommodated temporarily in the Primary School for the night and rehoused at various places in the town on the Sunday when vehicles were obtained to move furniture, much of which had been washed out by floods onto the street. In some houses the water remained at 4ft deep for some time. Not a house or shop on Freeman Street escaped. Many of the houses facing the recreation ground were found to have been torn in half by the force of the storm. A small saloon car was forced out of its garage and deposited in a crater caused by the flood.

The quayside at Wells on the morning after the great storm (*Gressenhall Farm and Workhouse Museum of Norfolk Life*)

Probably the most starling piece of debris left by the flood was Motor Torpedo Boat "Terra Nova" used by the local sea scouts. Wrenched from its moorings the 160 ton vessel

was left high and dry on the Quayside. Many other boats were wrenched and wrecked from their moorings while many shop fronts along the quay were badly damaged, after their windows had been smashed by the force of water and stock ruined by the flooding sea.

When the waters abated the damage to the surrounding countryside became clear. The coniferous forest planted and maintained by successive generations of Lord Leicester of Holkham Hall was is disarray, the popular tourist spot known as Abraham's Bosom was badly damaged by the waters. Wood fragments littered Beach Road along with animals, domestic effects and boats hung on and beside the trees and fences where they were deposited by the abating waters. In total about 1,000 acres of cultivated marsh and pasture was washed over by the sea and left with a "scoured" look caused by the deposits of dirty sand left on them. Farm animals took to dung heaps and hay stacks to evade the waters, by which means a number did survive, especially chickens.

It was estimated that about 1,000 sheep grazing on the marsh were lost, also many head of cattle, horses and pigs. Among the earliest tolls reported was that of 50 head of cattle lost by Mr E W Flint of Manor Farm Wells and 470 ewes, all in lamb, owned by Mr L G Harrison of Warham, most of these sheep carcasses ended up in flooded houses and outbuildings having drifted in on the flood waters. The clearing up and disposal (normally by burial) of the carcasses over the ensuing weeks is well remembered by those involved as one of the most repugnant tasks carried out after the floods. Incredibly, Mr Flints' cattle had in fact been frightened and had simply run away from the floods and found their way back over the next few days. One bullock ended up on Holkham Station. The station was surrounded by water, about 4ft in depth. Despite rescue attempts the distressed animal would not budge so a Mrs French took it upon herself to row out and take it fresh water and food and a few days later eventually got it out.

Dead cows on the embankment and flood waters cover the playing fields to the backs of the houses on Freeman Street, Wells.

Over the days immediately after the flood "Operation Sandbag and Shovel" was implemented by UDC workmen, troops and volunteers to plug the breeches in the sea defences. The new sewerage works at Wells had been totally submerged by the flooding sea water so it was not possible for the fire engines to do any useful pumping until the old sea

One of three breaches torn out by the surging flood waters along the embankment from the Wells Quay to the beach. This one, about half way along its length, scoured a hole 15ft deep and an acre in area. (*Gressenhall Farm and Workhouse Museum of Norfolk Life*)

Breach in the embankment near the old ship's channel for Holkham's Staithe and Abrham's Bosom. The waters surged through here and carried away the Jubilee Café. (*Gressenhall Farm and Workhouse Museum of Norfolk Life*)

Cutting a channel into a bank to let water drain away at Wells on 2 February 1953. (*Gressenhall Farm and Workhouse Museum of Norfolk Life*)

The MTB *Terra Nova* on Wells quayside 3 February 1953. A lasting reminder of the floods, for a while anyway, the MTB was relaunched on Wednesday 29 April by means of greased cylinders, on which it slid back into the water. Despite its ordeal *Terra Nova* was on an even keel and had sustained no serious damage.

The coast road at Morston under flood. When the tidal surge came the salt marshes offered no defence against the mighty wall of water.

wall had been repaired and defences tightened. Local fire pumps were joined by those of Lancashire County Fire Service to begin the pumping operation which began with a 96 hour continuous pumping operation to get the remaining flood waters in a manageable state. Although the land and forest reconstruction took many years many townsfolk of Wells came to celebrate the "end of the floods" in April 1953 when, before a crowd of over 2000, the "Terra Nova" was pushed back into the water from its "rest" on the Quayside.

BLAKENEY & WIVETON

When the sluice gates and bank at Morston broke under the pressure of the rising sea water shortly after 6.00pm on the night of 31 January 1953 a tidal wave swept up the River Stiffkey and overflowed the banks as it surged onwards. At Stiffkey the wall of water piled up against the low hump-backed bridge on the Stiffkey–Binham Road and swamped nearby buildings to a depth of two and a half feet. Luckily there were no casualties here and most folks pulled together to tackle the flood waters. At 5.00pm, about the same time as waters began to spill over the quayside at Wells, the tide began to lap the sea wall at Blakeney. Soon it was over the top and the banks rapidly gave way under the surging waters pouring thousands of tons of water over the marshes. At the same time the bank at the Cley end was breached bringing another inrush of water. Soon hundreds of acres of valuable grazing land became a mass of swirling muddy waters some 6ft deep.

One lucky escape was experienced by Mr H Dawson and his daughter Jill from "Woodside" Weybourne as they came down Blakeney Hill: "…seeing the water at the bottom I pulled up as quickly as I could but I had run the car up to the hub of the wheels. I jumped out and tried to start it again – then I heard Jill screaming "I'm drowning." By the time I got her out I was waist deep in water and we fled up the hill. We looked back but could see no sign of the car (above the water). I would say the water rose four feet in three minutes." The car was later recovered from Wiveton Marshes about 500 yards from where Mr Dawson and his daughter abandoned it.

As waters rose boats were torn from their moorings and smashed to matchwood. Others were carried on the rushing waters up the Glaven valley, some reaching as far as Glandford

Boats left stranded on the quayside at Blakeney. (*Gressenhall Farm and Workhouse Museum of Norfolk Life*)

This large boat was carried to the far side of the yard of the Blakeney Hotel on flood waters (*Gressenhall Farm and Workhouse Museum of Norfolk Life*)

where flood waters were recorded as deep as eight feet. Along the quayside the abating waters left a number of small boats in a line "like a row of ducks" entering the Blakeney Hotel. In the yard of the hotel three of the larger craft were thrown together and got jammed in so tightly and were only removed with the aid of an RAF crane a few days later. Most of the houses in the Westgate Street area were flooded to a depth of several feet and the wooden Quay Café was extensively damaged but fortunately there was no loss of life or serious injuries.

The view out to sea showing the salt marshes under flood along the embankment at Blakeney (*Gressenhall Farm and Workhouse Museum of Norfolk Life*)

Broken flint walls and stranded boats along the quayside at Blakeney (*Gressenhall Farm and Workhouse Museum of Norfolk Life*)

The flood level plaque for the 1953 floods is high above head height on the quayside at Blakeney.

Sadly the nearby settlement of Wiveton was not as fortunate. The breach was made by the surging waters through the 300 year old Dutch-built Wiveton Bank which protected the Glaven Valley. The first flooding occurred in the evening but the following morning tide threatened to cause further breaks in the embankments. These fears demanded the rescue of the elderly Canon and Mrs Foyster and Miss Ellingworth from their seaward home. Two ambulancemen and another helper were led by Miss Helen Barclay, a Wiveton resident (she lived at Glaven Lodge) who was Commandant of the Walsingham and Wells Voluntary Aid Detachment of the British Red Cross Society. Picking their way down a steep bank they entered the house which was in total darkness. Eventually Miss Barclay got the elderly people onto stretchers and with the help of the ambulance men and by using tables and furniture as stepping stones she brought them across the water and up the steep bank to safety.

The flood plain at Wiveton (*Gressenhall Farm and Workhouse Museum of Norfolk Life*)

Miss Barclay gave the Foysters and Miss Ellingworth a home at her own residence and for the next three weeks she opened her home to flood victims, including one nursing case. Her work did not cease there, as she arranged provision of hot meals, the issue of dry wood for fires and helped in the emergency clothing distribution at Wiveton and Cley. For her tireless actions Miss Barclay was awarded an MBE in the East Coast Flood honours list.

The tragedy at Wiveton was only discovered on the house to house search on Sunday 1 February. At the inquest on the Tuesday 3 February Lt William Anthony Crabbe, the 25 year old Medical Officer at Langham, stated at about 12.00 noon he was assisting Police Sergeant Chapman to recover the body of 75 year old Edie Dix from her home – "Willow Cottage." She was floating face downwards in one of the downstairs rooms of the cottage, it was clear she was trying to get upstairs when she was caught and drowned by the sudden inrush of water.

CLEY

Shortly after 6.00pm the waters poured over the Wiveton bank and flooded Cley. Just as locals were becoming aware of the encroaching waters under the doors of their homes the bank gave way and a wall of water smashed across the marshes into Cley. Mr W D High, a boot and shoe repairer gave this account to a reporter shortly after the flood:

"At about 6pm on Saturday the water started to run under the door. It got up to window height, we barricaded ourselves in but then it seemed to subside. We thought the worst was over but suddenly the water rushed in like a tidal wave. We just had time to rush

A Red Cross nurse rows up Mackrell's Hill at Cley to attend local welfare cases.

upstairs and get out of the way and let the flood take its course. The water rose up about seven stairs and the whole building was shaking. All we could hear downstairs was the crashes as furniture and crockery were smashed. We took the chest of drawers out and prepared for the worst. We planned to float in them but we realise now our position would have been hopeless."

Nineteen year old Gordon Lee of Newgate, known to many locals as "Buttercup Joe" was subjected to a horrifying ordeal in the floods. When the waters were first rising up across the marshland he went to release his parent's pigs from their allotment. Having rescued the piglets we went back for the sow. The water was already up to his welly boot tops when he heard a terrific roar: "All I could see when I turned round was water. It seemed to reach from the ground to the sky." He clambered lightning quick on top for his shed and spent the next three hours watching the waters rise lap about the corners of the shed roof.

Joe was eventually forced to grab a pole and clamber along it to the top of a nearby tree. His plight was noticed by the arriving rescue parties from Holt Division St John Ambulance, British Red Cross, joined later by military assistance from Weybourne AA Camp, RAF and USAAF. Rescue bids were made but the strength of the waters rendered such efforts impossible. Eventually the waters abated slightly and rescue vehicles were able to plough through the water rescuing people from upper windows and eventually "Joe" from his tree. As the ambulance proceeded to Joe one of the crew members recalled the sound on loud thuds from something falling on the roof of the vehicle. All became apparent as they dragged Joe in accompanied by tens of screaming rats! These little "monsters" had all been climbing up trees to escape the waters and fell on rescue vehicle roofs like verminous raindrops as they passed by.

A staff reporter from the *Norfolk Chronicle* toured Cley and Salthouse interviewing some of those affected and recorded some of the damage he saw on Monday 2 February:

" Mr K Gilpin, licensee of the King's Head told me it was about 6.30pm when the water

The handwritten sign valiantly declares 'Business as usual' with a few supplies for the relief effort on the steps of Rust's Ltd shop in Cley on 4 February 1953. (*Gressenhall Farm and Workhouse Museum of Norfolk Life*)

The sea flooding right over the coast road and at least half way up the speed restriction signs at Cley. (*Gressenhall Farm and Workhouse Museum of Norfolk Life*)

first started coming in to his pub. The electricity failed at 6.45 and the next thing they knew was that there was four feet of water in the downstairs rooms. It had broken in through the Smoke Room and Bar. His cellar was still full of water.

Mr Gilpin, like all the villagers I met, was in good spirits and told me that he had served as usual on Sunday night. He had been more fortunate than many others for he had managed to save most of his carpets and mats, which in most other homes I visited were ruined. [Author's Note: A year later when the King's Head was sold taken over by a new landlord the seats and tables in the bar were found to still bear traces of old dry seaweed and detritus from the flood.]

Mrs Burnett, landlady of the George Hotel, which suffered badly, told me of the suddenness of the flood "one minute the water was just trickling in and the next we were rushing upstairs." As they looked out of their bedroom window they could see the water lapping over the upstairs window sills of the cottages opposite which, I noticed were severely damaged. Mrs Burnett said she had lost eight barrels of beer which had "just floated away" but was hoping that the brewery would help them out "Everyone has been so kind" she added.

I left the George Hotel and walked out onto the main street again. The windows of the fish and chip shop were smashed. The walls of the bowling green had been battered to the ground and heaps of rubble and stones were lying on the reed strewn turf."

The scene at Newgate was not much better. The road to Newgate at the bottom of the Town Yard was still impassable for days after the flood. Mr R G Massingham, licensee of the Swallows Hotel said:

"The flood first reached here about 8pm. The water rose until it burst through the tap room door and swamped through the smoke room. By 11pm it was touching the lamp above the door of the house – about 8ft high. We were marooned upstairs until about 8am when we were rescued."

Like many of those rescued from this little village (and Salthouse – about 60 people in total) Mr Massingham's wife and child were evacuated to Weybourne Anti Aircraft Camp where they were housed in the MI room, cinema and NAAFI where they also had their meals. One abiding memory of those who stayed in the NAAFI building is the net of balloons which was suspended above them, which were to have been released at the Sergeant's Mess Ball that night. The clearing up job was immense but most able men folk stayed behind and aided by British and American servicemen attempted the clearing up operation over the next few days. To refresh the workers a mobile canteen was set up by the St John Ambulance and staffed by Capt J W C Harvey, Miss E M Breeze and cadets of the Blakeney St John Nursing Cadet Division (some of whom were only 12 or 13 years old.) In the first 10 days over 4,000 cups of tea were served.

The height of the flood waters around this sign at Cley give an indication of the depth of the flood waters in this area. (*Gressenhall Farm and Workhouse Museum of Norfolk Life*)

SALTHOUSE

At Salthouse the ancient shingle bank stood as little defence to the onslaught of the North Sea surge, the foaming waters smashed through and his this sleepy coastal village like an "ocean steam roller." Although the wind was howling a gale there really was no warning for the people of Salthouse. Within 30 minutes of the breach every house along the coast road was flooded and the waters rising that many had to flee their homes for their lives as the water not only filled the ground floors but poured into the upper stories of these little coastal cottages.

Mr Cliff Woodhouse ended up making a hole through the wall of an upstairs room to which he and his wife had gone and crawled through it to safety. Mrs Cooke thought she and her family (husband and children of 10 and 5) had "had it" when after running upstairs the stairs collapsed at their heels. Retreating to the furthest room on the top floor, the only room left to them, they sat out the storm watching furniture tossed on the waves in front their upper storey windows "It was howling, raining, blowing, the noise of the sea hitting the walls and bedroom windows...we made the children sleep as much they could, they didn't understand because they weren't very old...No light, no match, never had a torch even. I can't explain what it felt like. I felt sick, sick inside. I kept pacing up and down the little space we had. I kept peeping out, the garage, it just crumpled, like putting a piece of paper on the floor, it just crumpled up. You couldn't even close your eyes or shut your ears to it because it was too loud.

At about half past one my husband got a ladder. The water had gone back enough for us to jump. Some people into a council house up Cross Street, very kind of them."

Before the emergency services arrived on the scene a number of improvised rescues were carried out by villagers for their neighbours. One of the most notable was when Mr Leslie

Front line Norfolk. In a vision akin to the Blitz this is the devastation caused when the wall of water hit Salthouse. A total of thirty-three properties were destroyed in this one village. (*Gressenhall Farm and Workhouse Museum of Norfolk Life*)

Cook, Mr Fred Woodhouse and Mr Kenny Brown had rescued Mr Derek Howlett whose house was almost collapsing. They had managed to get a rope to him after foundering about in the icy water for a few minutes – "He was just about all in when we got to him," said Mr Woodhouse.

A rare survival is the rescue report sheet for the night of the flood from Holt St John Ambulance Division compiled by Divisional Officer B.W. "Billy" Elsden.

"9.35pm Message received from Holt police – sea walls broken at Cley – Ambulance and First Aid teams required at once – no 'phone communications – road partially blocked by trees.

Called Ambulance driver and sent messages to homes of all St John personnel.

Informed by Div Supt J T Briggs and suggested all equipment including Neal Robinson stretcher, should be sent.

9.45pm Ambulance and two teams away with all equipment, blankets, hot water bottles etc.

Went to cinema, saw manager who called out St John men, then himself and one man checked exits for any others as programme finished.

Reported to police two teams away – more, including Red Cross nurses, leaving in a few minutes.

Called Sheringham – asked them to cover Holt for ambulance. Also would they report to area Commissioner Day, suggest First Aid Party ready to come in if necessary.

10.50pm Two further parties away in cars. Men not already sent were told to stand by, and informed police that, given a few minutes warning, we were ready to open up Headquarters for use as a casualty centre.

Received report that Cley, Salthouse, Wiveton and Glandford flooded.

12.45am Message from Wiveton that Canon and Mrs Foyster (bedridden) – house flooded to bedrooms – could they be removed to house quarter mile away. Message passed to D/O B W Elsden when returning with other rescued persons.

12.50am Refreshments prepared for returning rescue parties

No 4 Party returned to Holt but went back immediately with police. Ambulance required at Salthouse.

4.00am No 1 Party returned until daylight, going back at 7.00am to relieve No 2 Party. Reserve Party also away at scene.

10.00am Ambulance returned to refuel – team to rest till 2pm. Ambulance taken back by No 4 Party.

Throughout emergency each team worked on their own initiative, rescuing people from houses, searching for casualties and carrying to nearest transport.

16 members worked a total of 224 hours.

Damage to equipment was small ie lost four rubber bottles, two straps, blankets torn. Superficial damage to ambulance."

The report sheet does not, however, record the gallant actions of Supt Briggs and D/O Elsden in the rescue of victims of the flood. Their story is compiled from the confidential St John reports on the flood rescues at Salthouse, their published citations and letters of endorsement from the Chief Constable of Norfolk Constabulary based on eye witness statements.

The rescue parties on the coast road at Salthouse were led by Div Supt J T Briggs assisted by his D/O "Billy" Elsden, they carried out house to house checks of flooded properties in Cley and Salthouse. At Salthouse, the houses adjoining the main road received the full tidal force and although involving personal danger due to risk of collapse, were searched by St John personnel. The state of many buildings meant that rescues could only be effected via upper storey windows or by smashing through the roof. The strength of the gale and the absence of any artificial light greatly hampered all rescue work.

D/O Elsden, who was soaked to the skin, discovered the Misses Susan and Pamela Lascalles who had taken refuge on the first floor of their house opposite Beach Road. The stairs had been washed away so Elsden saved the women by stacking furniture against the walls of the house and with the aid of two soldiers lifted them to safety.

Divisional Superintendent J. T. Briggs and Divisional Officer 'Billy' Elsden of Holt Division, St John Ambulance Brigade – the rescue heroes at Salthouse.

The St John draft citation concludes:

"The Unit under these two Officers has been highly praised by residents of the three parishes referred to. Their immediate action and determined demeanour on a 27 hour shift undoubtedly averted a much greater tragedy, particularly at Salthouse, which proved so vunerable and where nearly all the houses adjoining the coast road are now in ruins.

In considering recognition for individuals, it can be asserted that Div Supt Briggs undoubtedly displayed calm and astute leadership, ably backed by the brave actions and abilities of D/O Elsden as Second in Command."

Divisional Superintendent Briggs was recognised with a Queen's Commendation and D/O "Billy" Elsden received a British Empire Medal in the Flood Honours List.

Sadly one life was lost at Salthouse, a 73 year old lady named Hannah Rachel Middleton who lived at "Ridgeway" with her 78 year old retired farmer husband, John. Giving evidence at her inquest the tragic circumstances of her death were told. Mr Middleton said that between 6.30 and 7.00 on the Saturday night he and his wife were in their house together. His wife went to bed early. Shortly after this he told her that the sea was coming into the village. "She then got up and when we were in the downstair room the sea forced the front door in and this caught my wife and knocked her down...I pulled her out of the water and put her on the table but the next big wave took me out of the back window and my wife went out of the doorway before I could do anything. Her body was discovered in the early hours of Sunday morning laying by a tree in her back garden by a large search party led by PC Leonard Appleton of Kelling

The gallantry of the rescue teams at Salthouse could never be described as exaggerated, particularly when the village was surveyed after the deluge. The staff reporter of the *Norfolk Chronicle* who toured Cley and Salthouse on the Monday after the storm recorded these impressions:

"What I had seen of the wreckage at Cley hardly prepared me for the shock I received when I entered Salthouse. It seemed as though the village had been struck by high explosive. The sea had torn gaping holes in the sides of houses, doors were hanging loose, piles of bricks, rubble and household equipment lay everywhere.

The stout walls and higher ground of the Dun Cow allowed it to stand firm in the face of the flood but the marshes and the coast road that normally snakes around the pub are all under water.

Complete walls of houses lie in forlorn heaps covered by mud and seaweed.

The telephone kiosk near the post office was lying smashed on the ground, window frames, water tanks, pieces of sheds and other outhouses were lying scattered in unfenced gardens. A motor car was stranded at the back of what used to be the business premises of Mr S G Craske, a builder and decorator whose premises had been reduced to utter chaos."

An *EDP* reporter found Commander N G Parkinson, a civil engineer whose office and workshop were destroyed trying to unlock his safe which had been found 120ft away from his office in which it stood. He said the marks on his property showed that at one time there was 20ft of water on the coast road. He said the windows were blown outwards indication the water pressure created the same effect as an explosion.

The emergency services, civilian, British and American military received unanimous praise from the people of Cley and Salthouse. Servicemen assisted in the evacuation of families made homeless and old folks, women and children were taken to Weybourne Camp while able bodied men and troops were engaged in salvaging personal belongings of flood victims. Norfolk Fire Service joined the salvage work as well as pumping flood water away, pumped 77 domestic water wells and handled the supply of fresh water, along with American mobile water tanks, to the villages for several days. American Military snack bars were set up along with a St John mobile canteen manned by Brigadier Kent-Lemon and his team of helpers, this particular canteen worked from 9am to 6pm every day for a week after the flood. On the first Sunday after the flood they supplied 300 airmen working on a breach in the shingle gap with food and drink – helpers actually managed to get the whole mobile canteen out to the bank where the men were working.

The debris strewn coast road to Salthouse from the Kelling end, the day after the floods. The detritus left on the surface evinces how far the waters reached up the road at the height of the storm. (*Gressenhall Farm and Workhouse Museum of Norfolk Life*)

The immediate needs of the distressed people at both Cley and Salthouse were served with the best the services and voluntary organisations could supply. Salvaged furniture was stored in the church and any available hut and store. A local Emergency Relief Committee functioned at General Leach's Manor House up the hill from the chapel. Dr Norbury established a Medical HQ at 3, The Council Houses and because the only shop in the village had been ruined, soldiers erected a sectional summer house given to the parish for postal and food requirements.

Lorry loads of clothes and furniture were charitably sent under the Women's Voluntary Service Scheme from all over the country to help the flood relief effort. Cley St John Hall was used for distribution and storage of these gifts well into May. Other gifts are remembered coming from Women's Institute, Australian Women's Guild, the Methodist Church, The Royal Antedeluvian Order of Buffalos and even a carpet sent for every house from Canada. Sir Thomas Cook, the County Commissioner of Norfolk St John Ambulance kept in close touch with all the relief efforts right down to being instrumental in obtaining several truck loads of "Coaloids" patent fuel to build the fires in the grates to assist in the drying out process for the restorable properties. Sadly many houses were beyond salvage in fact 33 houses were completely destroyed and some 20 damaged beyond repair – some families simply lost everything except their lives and the clothes they stood in.

The local gentry played their role too, Mrs Helen Knott of The Hall was confronted on the night of the flood with 200 men, women and children in various states of attire, wet and dry who had left their homes and sought refuge at the hall. Mrs Knott immediately gave her house over to become a relief centre, a purpose it served for the next three weeks as people found temporary accommodation with friends, family, at the disused Stiffkey Army Camp or in caravans loaned from local holiday camps and charitable people. Mrs Knott's efforts were supplemented by the contribution of Major Hubert Blount MC of Cley Old Hall. Despite his own house being partially flooded he loaned his secretary to the flood relief committee and assisted Mrs Knott in the facilitation of the St John Ambulance flood effort in the area including the temporary community centre established in the village school, staffed by St John nurses and local volunteers.

The work of sealing the large gap in the Salthouse bank began on Sunday 1 February under the supervision of Commander Parkinson, the local civil engineer who despite having his premises severely damaged by floods got straight to work on organising the rebuilding the sea defences. Flying Officer Stansel was in charge of 300 airmen who assisted with the bitterly cold work. Searchlights trained on the gap from the radar station enabled five bulldozers to continue banking the shingle up through the Tuesday night, but on Wednesday afternoon they were forced to retire by the heavy seas. The bank appeared to have been breached again and the St John canteen was hurriedly withdrawn to higher ground at the manor but luckily the waters abated before any serious breach occurred.

SHERINGHAM & CROMER

The popular coastal resort towns of Cromer and Sheringham had learnt from the bitter experience of severe encroachments by the sea in the past, especially Cromer where the old fishermen talked of the town of Shipdam which stood beyond the town and now washed over by the sea. When the weather was turning for the worse they said the bells of Shipden's submerged church of St Peter could be heard booming below the waves.

Great chunks of the land around Sheringham and Cromer were still being gouged out well into the 19th century so as their popularity as coastal resorts grew so did the ingenuity

Workmen repairing the badly damaged Sheringham promenade. (*John Childs*)

and investment in sea defences. Work began in Cromer in 1894 and given greater resolution in 1897 when the jetty was wrecked a grand scheme to connect East and West Esplanades and a sea wall was completed in 1901 for the grand sum of £34,000. A similar scheme was begun at Sheringham, by 1896 over £30,000 had been expended, by 1901 the sea wall and promenade extended two thirds of a mile, extended another 113 yards on the eastern side in 1909. Following the 1912 floods a raised promenade and shelter were also constructed. Thus when the North Sea serge hammered into these towns the defences and seafront took the brunt and the shops and dwellings of the towns were saved but this does not mean local folks were away from danger.

A thirty yard stretch of Sheringham promenade was torn away, large blocks of concrete were left laying around like toy bricks. When the waters abated and the Leas incline was found badly split half way down. The east end of the sea front had the worst buffeting. The wooden shelter near the "60 Steps" was smashed and the tank shelter given a severe battering on its seaward side. A large section of the Mo bandstand wall was torn away and the Little Mo, recently purchased by the UDC suffered badly. Part of the sea wall was washed away and a fishing boat was lifted onto a wall rear the Fisherman's Gangway. The lifeboat house doors were torn off but no damage was done to the lifeboat or the slipway – the lifeboat was on service again on Tuesday 3 February.

Winds drove water high over the sea walls and cliff-top hotels suffered water breaking through the roof or hurtling down their chimneys. The greatest danger here was from the roof tiles and chimney stacks being torn down onto the street below. Only one person was permanently evacuated from his sea soaked council cottage on the East Cliff. An eight month old baby was rescued from a house overlooking the Fisherman's Slipway at the West End by a police constable who put the child into a suitcase to protect it from flying tiles and pebbles.

Many hundreds of crushed and dead pilchards and lobsters were washed up at Sheringham after the storm. Local fishermen shook their heads, one is recorded saying "they are the ones that we put back over the side last year because they were too small." Now washed up and killed in such numbers great concern was shown by the fishermen that there would be a shortage that season. When uncertainty reigned at the costs of repairing the damage figures in excess of £150,000 were suggested. Mr F G Jordan the Chairman of Sheringham Council said "It is a catastrophe for Sheringham. It might take several years to recover."

Like Sheringham the town of Cromer was not flooded but the winds blew havoc across the town taking slates off roofs and blowing in some windows, including the large plate glass window at Mutimer's Store on Garden Street, the stand on Cromer's football field was also seriously damaged. The most serious human casualty was Mr Denis Robinson, a local businessman who suffered injuries to his ribs on the Saturday night when he was struck by a beach hut roof on Cromer sea front. It was hardly surprising to find worst of the damage was inflicted on the sea front. A vital groyne on the east end of the promenade was simply washed away by the force of the water. Much of the promenade sea defences were pulverised and the chalets behind had many of their windows smashed and most of their contents carried away on the tide with their doors.

Below left: Poor old Cromer pier took a real battering in the floods as its wood and concrete decking were torn up by the waves.

Below right: The rear roof of the Cromer Pier shops were completely smashed away (*Keith Skipper*)

The coping on the sea wall was badly damaged, the worst of it seemed to be just east of the pier and part of the slope near the Regency Hotel had begun to slip. A large chunk of cliff had been washed away between the East Prom and Happy Valley. The Café at the Runton end of the beach had its glass front shattered. The concrete path near the café was barred to the public because its foundations had been washed out. Beach hut proprietors were shocked to find every hut had been washed away together with stacks of deck chairs. The only hut still standing but badly battered was the St John Ambulance first aid post while lamp standards stood or laid in grotesque positions – mute testimony to the fantastic strength of the wind and sea.

The greatest concern was shown for Cromer's beloved pier. A great deal of the Pier decking, both wood and concrete had been washed away and there was a big gap between the pier entrance buildings and the Pavilion Theatre . The roof of the entrance buildings on the seaward side had been completely ripped away. The entire west side of the Pavilion Theatre had been ripped out. The pier girders at the north west corner of the pavilion had been twisted into all shapes and much of the decking ripped up and washed away. One eye witness who visited the theatre shortly after the storm recorded the scene:

"The stage inside the Pavilion looked like a giant scenic railway and the seating, some of it gone, lay piled up. A good deal of the Pavilion flooring had gone and sea sprayed through it at times. From appearances it looked as if the whole of the dressing rooms and stage would have to be rebuilt and that part of the west roof would have to be taken down before the support girders could be straightened."

Above left: Some of the walls of the Pavilion Theatre at the end of the pier had been destroyed while the girders and structures within had been warped by the force of water in such a way it was said to resemble a 'scenic railway.' (*Keith Skipper*)

Above right: The RNLI boathouse at Cromer pier head also received a battering that lifted the lifeboat, *Henry Blogg*, off its keel-way and smashed it onto the side of the boathouse. (*Keith Skipper*)

At the pier's seaward end the lifeboat shed, from which the legendary Coxswain Blogg and his crew launched so many times, had almost been swept away. The doors were ripped away and the lifeboat – named after the great skipper – having been lifted off its keelway by the powerful waters, smashed into the side of the boathouse and was left listing forlornly to its port side.

Cromer folks were determinedly not going to be beaten. The lifeboat was officially on service again in her damaged boathouse the following Wednesday. Workmen lifted her back into the keel-way and inspection revealed negligible damage. Work on the sea front and the damaged groyne at the east end employed every available council worker, aided by ten temporary labourers and as much equipment as possible was salvaged from the pier Pavilion. The pier itself was restored by 1955 but Cromer was not without entertainment – the end of the pier summer show "Out of the Blue" was moved to the Parish Hall which had been converted at lightening speed by Cromer Council into the "Summer Theatre". Mr R W Graveling declared at the meeting of the Town Council "I would like it to go out that we are determined to do all we possibly can to get the place back in order for the season." A view echoed by Mr R T Kidd who said they should use the wartime motto "business as usual."

Forty years on local crabmen still recall the night they hauled their boats to the top of the Gangway and watched anxiously as waves swept up the steep cobbled causeway to within feet of where they stood.

Part of Cromer promenade wrecked by the wall of water that hit it. (*Keith Skipper*)

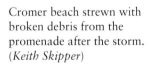

Cromer beach strewn with broken debris from the promenade after the storm. (*Keith Skipper*)

Tarmac and concrete pulverised by the force of water in the teeth of the storm. The chalets behind were also assaulted with windows and interior fittings smashed and their doors carried away by the tide.

MUNDESLEY, BACTON, WALCOTT & HAPPISBURGH

These quiet coastal villages have always had a respectful relationship with the sea. The fishermen fished the waters and their beaches drew holidaymakers in the summer while the sea took its toll by claiming "bites" of land from the cliffs around them. Over the years as land was gradually eaten away the villages steadily moved inland and re-established themselves, the last major storms to adversely effect this area were in the middle of the nineteenth century – in 1836 and 1845.

Kindly neighbours assist in the evacuation of Mr. Suckling's furniture and effects from his beleaguered home, Marine House at 'The Dell', Mundesley, 1 February 1953.

On 31 January 1953 the sea defences at Mundesley took the brunt of the seas' onslaught at about 8.15pm; by 9pm the waves were striking the sea walls and rising to about 80ft. serious breaches in the cliffs were caused between The Dell and Cliff House. The sea wall supporting the promenade was too weak to stand up to this pounding and was undermined at the east end and the concrete promenade ended up being smashed up "as though it were so much hardboard." Mr C. C. Payne's Cliffside Café and Shop known to many holidaymakers was smashed to matchwood, the beach huts were simply washed away and Mr Ketteringham's store huts and the St John Ambulance beach first aid hut totally destroyed.

In The Dell the waves undermined the cliff edge beneath Marine House leaving this building poised over the cliff with a drop of over 15ft. The owner, Mr E. Suckling, was in Cambridge when the waves hit but his property was cleared the following day by willing neighbours. Two doors away lived Mrs Haworth. She was in her bedroom at about 9pm when she happened to be looking out of the window. Suddenly she saw what looked like a mountain of water rushing at the house. She shouted to her husband and as she did so the huge wave struck the gable end of their house. Looking out of the window, to her astonishment, she saw the wave take away the front of Mr Suckling's house. Mr Suckling later spoke of the help given by local people. Mr Harry Mason and his wife, together with Mr Grey from next door stayed up all night to keep watch and then organised a rescue team in the morning to save the remaining contents of the house that were kindly stored by Mr Ward at The Lifeboat Inn.

In the week preceding the deluge local newspapers covered the dangerous situation of Beach Cottage which, due to coastal erosion now stood only a few yards from the cliff edge at Cable Gap, Bacton. The local council had granted Mrs A J Plaister, the cottage's owner, £50 for earth to help fill up over some faggots Mrs Plaister said she would dump in front of her house in an attempt to build some sort of sea defence. The wall of water hit Bacton shortly after Mundesley on the night of 31 January and reached the houses situated about 100 yards from the cliff top about 8.30pm. When the new day dawned only a few loose bricks remained to show Beach Cottage ever existed. Bacton lost about 30 yards of its low cliff and a number of buildings, mostly from the Cable Gap area. With the loss of the cliff half of the road that road ran between Cable Gap along the cliff to the bungalow estate also disappeared.

Close by Beach Cottage was another owned by Mrs Thornilow of Ridlington, which was also swept away complete with its furnishings. Opposite here stood a wooden construction, the property of Mr F. W. Edwards the well-known North Walsham baker. From here he served refreshments in the summer months nothing of this building remained, not even the ground it stood on as the cliffs had been gouged a full 30 yards at this point. Gone too was another bungalow the property of Mr Chittock of North Walsham. Mr Chittock's tall horse drawn caravan which was a known landmark for cycle tourists in the area was found laid on its side crushed by the waves.

Prior to the deluge the "Hermitage," property of Mr D Gordon, a Norwich market trader stood some 60ft from the cliff edge. On the Sunday the building was found to be just a few feet from the edge and the entire lower floor, which had been flooded, a foot deep in mud. With the combined effort of Mr Gordon's family and villagers they loaded what furniture and belongings they could and evacuated their home.

The elderly Miss R Rees of Ash Cottage is remembered for industriously scraping the thick sandy mud from the floors, walls and furniture of her bungalow the following morning in a proud attempt to clean her home into something habitable. Tragically her story was a familiar one in this area of coast, her home was now too close to the sea for safety and she would soon have to leave and find somewhere else to live. Before the North Sea surge her home was well clear of the cliff edge. Beyond her back door was a little garden, a full sized tennis court backed by a high bank and thick hedge. Beyond that was a road and then three Cliffside summer bungalows, Mrs Ress was reduced to half a tennis court and a house full of slimy mud.

During the night of the storm she was alone listening to the storm when the water rushed in and "a black swirling torrent" filled her home. The back door and windows were hammered on "I thought it was thunder but it was the bungalows over the road falling into the sea." She was then gathered up in the arms of Mr Y E Thompson, a retired schoolmaster who carried her to his nearby home for safety. A good deed he extended to another neighbour, 87 year old Mrs Channing of Cliff Cottage. The back door to her home "Cliff Cottage" almost opened directly over the cliff edge the following morning.

Further along the village several bungalows of the Seaview Estate were swept into the sea and a fleet of caravans well behind the cliff were found to be axle deep in water on Sunday morning. Numerous properties in Bacton were damaged by the storm. It is somewhat ironic to note at the Smallburgh RDC meeting the preceeding week the erection of sea defences along the coast. The proposed scheme to defend Walcott had just been approved to reach along to Bacton!

When the waters abated insult was given to injury when on the afternoon of Sunday 1 February the 4,000 ton tanker *Olcades* beached at Bacton. No one on board and lifeboats gone it was thought the boat had broken lose while on tow to the breakers crossing the North Sea. With the change of tide the tanker drifted down to the Ostend end of Walcott, bows directed at and about 30 yards off the cliff and firmly embedded in the sand. It was doubtful there would ever be enough high water to refloat her. For some locals it was the final straw – surrounded by the detritus and destruction of the flood some folks complained in no uncertain terms to the local authorities about "that bloody eyesore boat!"

The storms of December 1952 had gouged away the soft cliffs dangerously close to the coast road at Walcott.

Above left: During the storm of 31 January 1953 a large section of the low cliffs and coast road were destroyed at Walcott.

Above right: The anti-tank blocks left over from the Second World War absorbed the force of the wall of water and the fierce crash of the waves saving a number of premises from complete destruction of the seafront at Walcott.

The small coastal settlement of Walcott had received a real pounding from the sea in December 1952 where the sea defences were torn away to within feet of the main coast road. A new defensive wall was erected "with more haste than discretion" but it was not only inadequate it was not completed when the wall of water hit. Before the floods Walcott looked very similar to some of the small coastal settlements of West Norfolk with its rows of wooden bungalows and holiday cottages. If there had been a USAAF base nearby the chances were a disaster comparable to that of Snettisham, Heacham or Hunstanton could have happened here. Fortunately there was no base nearby and most of the holiday bungalows were unoccupied for the coastal bungalows bore the brunt of the water and their wreckage was strewn for a mile along the cliff edge.

The morning after the sea surge the main coast road through Walcott was found to have simply disappeared, the lack of adequate, complete defences meant the road, along with sixty feet of cliffs and dozens of bungalows and chalets stood no chance against the waves. Standing bleak and stark against the wreckage was St Helen's, the roadside café which stood on the landward side of the road and looked in danger until the road undermined in December was repaired. After the flood this poor building stood with its bay windows overhanging the cliff and sand fifteen feet below.

Above left: Wreckage of wooden chalets and bungalows after the storm at Walcott(*Gressenhall Farm and Workhouse Museum of Norfolk Life*)

Above right: After the sea bit into the cliffs at Happisburgh and the home of Miss C. P. Charter was left hanging over the cliff edge. (*Gressenhall Farm and Workhouse Museum of Norfolk Life*)

Left: The view from the low cliff of Walcott after the floods and the 4,000 ton tanker *Olcades* that had been washed ashore.

What did stand of the coastal wall was praised by some locals. Mr W D Murphy, who occupied the General Stores and Post Office maintained that had it not been for the new wall, aided no doubt by some of the old wartime block sea defences, his wooden building would not be standing! As it transpired all of these buildings were demolished soon after as a new sea wall, coast road and shops were constructed – a little further inland!

In the 1830s it was predicted that Happisburgh Church would succumb to coastal erosion in the next 100 years. Many locals thought these floods would prove to be a death knoll for one of the most distinctive landmarks of the North East Norfolk coast but residents of this pleasant coastal village breathed a sigh of relief as they emerged from their homes after the storm to see the ancient monument standing tall and proud as ever. No flooding came to Happisburgh – its tall cliffs saw to that, but at a cost. The only notable property damage was to the Beach Road residence of Miss C P Charter, her house was already close to the cliff edge and the storm swept away her garage and wrecked her bungalow with the fall of a cliff. It soon became clear that the sea had claimed an average of 30 ft of cliff had been scoured away all along the seaward side of Happisburgh. Geologists later commented that far more might have collapsed had it not been for the solid layer of clay that founds them.

The view after the wall of
water hit the Beach Road
end of the little village of
Sea Palling. (*Gressenhall
Farm and Workhouse
Museum of Norfolk Life*)

SEA PALLING

Sea Palling was, for hundreds of years, a simple, sleepy fishing village on the North East
coast of Norfolk. With the holiday trade booming at Great Yarmouth and seaside
entertainments at Hemsby this little village had but simple facilities for the visitor who
may have fancied a trip or few days by the sea and sandy dunes. The summer-time visitor
would no doubt recall the Beach Road which literally led to the seaside; as the
macademised road surface ran into the sands at the top of the road. At this end of the
village were the visitor facilities consisting of the small restaurant, cafe, general store,
bakery and the flint faced Lifeboat Inn. Not just a tourist pub The Lifeboat was in many
ways the hub of village life with a classic traditional pub interior and, on the right night,
shanties sung by local fisherman.

The first inkling of the impending flood came as early as quarter to eight when the first
trickling water found its way over the dunes and onto Beach Road. Residents of the area
assumed it was merely a slight overflow or the gathering of spray from the dashing waves.
Above all there fleas no need to panic. At Sea Palling there was no sea wall the only defence
between the village and the sea were the sand dunes and marrams. Even this "defence"
had a weak point where they were crossed by a well worn footpath that was also used as
a passage to drag boats on and off the beach. About 8.15pm the North Sea surge hit Sea
Palling and blew a huge gap through the sandy dunes and poured into the seaward dwelling
of the village killing seven.

At the inquest Mr Albert John Fox spoke his horrific ordeal on that fateful night. The cottage where he lived with his wife Doris (42) their six month old baby Edwin Eric Fox and her two children by a former marriage, Stephen and Merle Wilmott, aged thirteen and eight respectively, was a mere 30 yards from The Gap and received the full force of the wall of water. When Mr Fox noticed water had begun to trickle under his front door (which faced landward) his eldest son Stephen ran to the back door which faced Beach Road. As soon as he opened the door the water poured into the kitchen. Mr Fox ran and forced the door shut and sent the children upstairs. Within a few minutes the water was knee high in the house.

Looking out from an upstairs widow they saw the water was five feet high and was "racing in a whirlpool fashion" coming down the road and round the house. By 9pm the water was up to the downstairs ceiling in the Fox's home. Mr Fox said he heard the back door break away and shortly afterwards the front one also collapsed. At about 10pm Mrs Fox shouted out of her bedroom window to her neighbour Mrs Sarah Clarke (who also died that night). Five minutes later he heard the outhouse go and immediately afterwards the café close by began breaking up. This lowered the water in the garden considerably and knowing high tide was just about over they decided to sit tight in their house.

The next series of event are recorded in Mr Fox's own words:

"The gable end of the house fell out and I could see the tremendous waves coming down through the Gap and sweeping past down Beach Road. I had already tied the baby to my back in a pillow slip and tied Merle with a sheet to her mother's waist. I prepared a rope from blankets which I lowered out of the bedroom window and we went down it. Sand had piled up where I landed in front of my house. My wife dropped Merle and then followed herself. I helped Stephen down and whilst doing so part of the house fell on us cutting Stephen and myself.

We worked towards the other end of the cottages and on reaching there my wife slipped and fell into the water. I picked her up and helped her back to the shelter of the wall but I was caught by a wave coming through an open door and was carried across to a cottage 15 yards away. I lost my balance and was carried another 30 yards into a hedge which I was making for. I regained my feet but found that the baby had been washed away.

Meanwhile the other three had been able to work their way down the hedge and rejoin me. After a breather we went further down the hedge with the object of getting to the Coastguard Cottages. I found that the current was too strong to cross over so decided to remain in the safety of the hedge."

About two and a half hours later they were still in the hedge but owing to the bitter wind Merle had lost consciousness and the other two were little better. The water was beginning to recede. Mr Fox said he had tied a cycle lamp about his wife's neck and this being switched on no doubt attracted some of the rescuers. Two firemen, Sidney William Lancaster (Officer in Charge) and Arthur Dixon of the Stalham Fire Brigade told the coroner of their discovery of the Fox family in the flood waters. Seeing the disaster which confronted them Mr Lancaster had gone to the nearby Broads village of Hickling to fetch a boat to fetch a boat to aid the rescue work. It was found impossible to row the boat against the tide so the firemen waded through the water pushing the boat and clinging

Below: The gaunt ruin of what was the Lifeboat Inn at Sea Palling (*Gressenhall Farm and Workhouse Museum of Norfolk Life*),

Bottom: One of the cars found submerged in sand after the flood waters abated at Sea Palling (*Gressenhall Farm and Workhouse Museum of Norfolk Life*).

Beach Restaurant and wrecked houses at the top of Beach Road, Sea Palling. A number of lives were lost when the wall of water hit here. (*Gressenhall Farm and Workhouse Museum of Norfolk Life*)

Local people taking stock of the flood damage at Sea Palling.

Sergeant Archie Burrell of North Walsham Division, St John Ambulance Brigade was the senior ambulance-man present at Sea Palling during the rescue operations.

The Cock Inn at Sea Palling, 1953

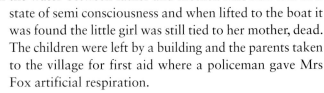

to its sides – swimming where the depth of water meant their feet could not touch the ground.

Behind the Beach Café was a light and on making their way there they found Mr Fox crouched on the bank. His wife was in the water three feet deep, her head and shoulders above and the boy lying dead in the water between father and mother. Mrs Fox was in a state of semi consciousness and when lifted to the boat it was found the little girl was still tied to her mother, dead. The children were left by a building and the parents taken to the village for first aid where a policeman gave Mrs Fox artificial respiration.

A call had already been made for an ambulance to attend casualties caused by flooding at Sea Palling. The confidential report compiled by Divisional Superintendent George Burton "GB" Fuller of North Walsham St John Ambulance Division is published below:

"At 12.20am Sergeant Archie Burrell was given the message that an ambulance an crew were requested to attend the floods at Sea Palling. The ambulance picked him up at 12.30am. On arrival at Palling Sergt Burrell reported at the Cock Inn as instructed.

Mrs Fox had only just been brought in, she was lying

on the bar table covered with only a wet rag and a blanket [Author's note: As her children got colder in the water Mrs Fox had wrapped them in her own clothing.]. A police constable was doing artificial respiration and Sergt Burrell fetched warm blankets from the ambulance and continued the treatment, but she died shortly after."

Another account given at the inquest was that of retired RAF Officer Arthur Cook aged 52 who lived at "Homestead" on Beach Road. After identifying his mother and father in law, Isabella and William Hamblin aged 80 and 87 respectively, both of Beryl Cottage, Mr Cook stated he returned to the village from Norwich shortly after 8.15pm. He was told of the breach in the Gap. He left home and went to see his mother and father in law. In the gale and sleet and snow he found headway difficult. He stopped to warn the patients of the nursing home en route. When he came out the current was exceptionally strong.

He was compelled to leave Beach Road and make his way along another route. On the way he went to Coastguard Cottages and mounting a bank made his way to Beryl Cottage. He was unable to reach the door to get to his relatives owing to debris having accumulated between another house and theirs causing the water to rise very rapidly. Mr Cook's testimony continued:

"I saw my father in law at the back door in answer to my call and I urged him to get upstairs with mother as soon as possible. It was impossible to get to them as in addition to sweeping directly down the street the water had turned and was surging past the side of the house facing the sea."

Mr Cook said he saw torch flashes from his father in law at the bedroom window to assure him his father in law had got there. Mr Cook then returned via open fields to warn people of the danger and made another attempt to reach Beryl Cottage. He made little ground as furniture was coming down the road with the tide and a wall collapsed in front of him. Once more he was forced to return and warn people.

It was not until 3am that he got up Beach Road to find complete devastation. The three houses in which his father and mother in law, Mrs Clarke and Mrs Fox lived appeared to have been completely washed away.

The first emergency call from Sea Palling was rung through to the police station at North Walsham at 8.50pm. Supt William Garner together with his son and PC Denney left immediately through snow and gale force winds for the stricken village. On arrival Garner was told that there were people in houses at the sea end of Beach Road but nothing could be done because all the boats had been washed away. Soon joined by other local bobbies; PC Medford and Sgt Stevenson they made their way towards the beach. First along a roadside bank, the top of which was above water. Supt Garner takes up the story:

"At the end of the bank we linked hands and waded up the road to our waists in water. We managed to get as far as the last house on the right next to the Golden Beach Restaurant. Conditions became very difficult; we were getting the full force of the wind, the water got deeper and we were feeling the effects of the big waves pouring through the breach in the marrams which was then about 75 yards wide. PC Denney was blown over and we grabbed him and pulled him up.

We got to a wall to which we were able to cling and got in difficulties with brick rubble under our feet and telegraph poles above our heads. Holding to the wall we had a good look round and could see persons in the bedrooms of their houses at the windows. At that time all the houses we could see were intact. We decided that the people were safer in their upstair rooms than they would be if we got any of them out and decided to leave rescue attempts until the tide began to ebb. We shone our torches on the different windows in order to let people know that help was near and to reassure them."

Supt Garner left the flood danger area and set up a control centre at the Cock Inn. After telephoning for the North Walsham Ambulance and police reinforcements he arranged for the pub to remain open with drinks and fires and arranged for the Church Rooms to be heated and prepared as a temporary reception centre. He also requested aid from RAF Coltishall who answered with 90 officers and men on the scene within the hour.

At 1.30am news came back to control from the fire brigade boat rescue parties that some of the houses had collapsed and people were dead and dying. Taking available personnel to the Beach Road area they arrived just as Mr and Mrs Fox were being got out and taken to the Cock and the two children placed against the café.

Supt Garner continues; "At the sea side of the café, where the Hamblins had lived, we found the section of the house had collapsed and among the debris, under a smashed iron bedstead I found Mr Hamblin. He was dead. We searched for his wife but could not find her then.

Some of the walls of the Lifeboat Inn had fallen out and also the walls of another house nearby. We could see people in the upper rooms and they were rescued. We got a family of eight from the house next to the Beach Restaurant and carried them up."

The report of North Walsham Ambulance states: "Supt Garner asked Sergt Burrell if he could get a family of eight, who were all in a very distressed condition to Maddison's holiday camp at Hemsby. He had the wheel stretcher and other equipment removed from the ambulance and left with Cpl William Taylor. On return from Hemsby another load of five patients were ready to go and Cpl. Taylor was sent in charge."

At 4.30am the police went in again with RAF personnel and Dr Walsh. The water had then subsided and there were high patches of dry sand around the buildings. On one of these sand patches near the restaurant Supt Garner found the partly clothed body of Mrs Hamblin. It was intended to leave evacuation of the nursing home until daybreak but at about 6am the water appeared to be coming in again. "Supt Garner and Sergt Burrell decided they could not afford to wait for the return of the ambulance before evacuating the patients. Garner and Burrell, assisted by available personnel, got the patients down by using the ambulance carrying sheet and poles, tearing up pillow cases to tie them in. The patients were placed in an RAF lorry which was run through the water and door level and five were later brought to North Walsham hospital."

As the waters abated and in the daylight of Sunday the terrible damage inflicted on Sea Palling was revealed. The 100 yard breach gaped wide and ominous between the marrams. Sea water stretched in lakes and great puddles, some up to hip depth, across the neighbouring low-lying fields. Sand was left where it had been washed up around the wrecked and damaged houses, piled up to the tops of doors in places. Tractors and boats manned by willing neighbours chugged around the area moving salvaged furniture to safe storage as inhabitants assisted by RAF personnel searched their damaged homes for what was left of their personal possessions. It seemed like every local person came back to help digging sand out of rooms which seemed to contain little else. Even small children with spades helped them.

Before the flood the end of Beach Road went narrowly to the sea flanked on either side by buildings. After the flood this area now fanned out into a wide open vista and had spread 300 yards up the road towards the village reaching a depth 5ft in places. The roofs were all that were visible of two cars buried in sand and detritus. The *EDP* reporter who visited the area noted one vignette: "Rubbish, which was once somebody's furniture, surrounds a notice which ironically threatens a £5 fine for littering the beach." Ash's Restaurant still stood, in part, half filled with sand and its windows smashed, from it was defiantly flown a white ensign put there by Mr Doug Ash as he hoped to salvage what remained of his business and caravan site. Beside Ash's stood The Longshore Café and opposite the restaurant stood a bakery shop. When the marrams gave way these shops took the full force of the onslaught and in the morning not a brick or remnant remained to indicate where they stood before the waters came.

The Lifeboat Inn had been reduced to a shell. The Beach Road side of the pub was torn away and sand piled up to the ceiling within while incredibly the outbuildings and lavatory remained standing although filled with about 4ft of sand. Opposite stood the pathetic remnants of the Hamblin's and Mrs Clarke's cottages. Beyond that, the last vestige between land and sea was an old-fashioned caravan with a chimney in which lived Mr Bertie Feathers, brother of the Lifeboat's publican, who stuck in his little wooden home until forced to leave by the police. All the while he maintained his home would be safe – and it was!

Soon bulldozers and RAF teams were on the scene to plug the breaches that still left the village vulnerable to the threatening of the sea. Following direct orders from the Home Secretary, Sir David Maxwell Fife, a full emergency scheme between Services and civilians was put into action. At noon on Tuesday 150 RAF and Naval personnel from RAF Stations Coltishall and West Raynham arrived and under the leadership of Flt Lt P. Harrison.

Immediately setting to work they were soon joined by local volunteers and by four o'clock a three foot wall closed the breach, sealing off the open sea. Meanwhile civilians operating five bulldozers piled the sand onto the landward side of the wall to form a huge buttress.

Over the next few days the Sea Palling sand bag sea defence wall grew to a height of twelve feet. With the realisation that over and eight mile area either side of Palling other breaches had to be sealed. An appeal for public assistance by Alan E Crisp the Clerk of Smallburgh RDC saw 2000 volunteers descend on this battered coastal village as it became the nerve centre for the co-ordination of these public volunteers and about 700 service personnel all at work, often in bitterly cold winds, filling sandbags and labouring hard to make this strip of coast safe again.

By this time Beach Road was a mass of slimy mud, compared to the quags of the Western Front in the Great War. Parts of the land on either side were still partially immersed in water and diggers were carving out dykes to release the larger "lakes." The *Norfolk Chronicle* reporter described the area of the breach nearly a fortnight after the deluge:

"The sight of the sea is cut off completely by the now twenty foot wall of sandbags and heaped sand, Very little of the workers can now be seen from the Beach Road, the bulk of the effort being concentrated on the seaward side of the dunes. Immediately below the sand bag wall and to either side as far as the eye can see, hundreds of men are working to build a second wall some yards from the second inner wall. As they do a line of bulldozers all along the beach are pushing sand up against it. To the Eccles end of the Gap, the River Board have ordered the erection of five groynes."

Behind the dunes to the landward side a great deal of the rubble has been cleared. Standing beside the shell of the restaurant a field kitchen had been erected by the RAF to provide beverages for the men. Tea was made on the spot but soup, made at the school

Struggling to fill the gap in the dunes at Sea Palling on the third day after the flood. It had been suggested that the next tide would be a repeat of the last and national servicemen, many of them from the RAF, were drafted in and worked through bitterly cold nights filling sandbags and building an improvised wall to plug the gap. They were joined in their efforts by civilian volunteers from all over Britain who came to help.

further in the village was reheated in the field so it could be served up piping hot. Across what was Beach Road the army have a similar arrangement, only instead of erecting a shelter they commandeered what was left of the Lifeboat Inn. Together with this, to provide for the civilians, the Education Committee, had an emergency food service in their role with the Civil Defence stationed two vans with "two pretty WRAFs" serving hot tea and eats for the volunteers. Next door to this in a house previously occupied by a family with 7 children the Royal Corps of Signals detachment made their headquarters. Led by a corporal the four soldiers had established living quarters and a switchboard with a radio

Dr. E. Lincoln Ralphs, Norfolk's Emergency Meals Officer, with soldiers drafted in to deal with the civil emergency opening tins of soup concentrates to help feed those who had lost their homes and those who toiled on the sandbag wall.

truck on hand (in case of failures) in contact with Norwich HQ and other sections along the Sea Palling and Waxham operational area.

With a strong military presence and hundreds of volunteers the breaches were blocked and made safe from sea encroachments by the weekend of February 14/15 and the people of Sea Palling could look to rebuilding their little village again. In the flood honours list Supt Garner of North Walsham Police was awarded and MBE and Sub Officer S W Lancaster a BEM for their courage, quick thinking, rescue work and control of the situation on the night of the flood. Mr Arthur Cook, the brave civilian who risked his life to warn his neighbours and neighbouring family members received a Queen's Commendation. In an official letter of thanks from Norfolk's Chief Constable the following members of the Stalham Fire Brigade were mentioned as having done "exceedingly good work," they were:

Sidney William Lancaster (in charge)
Arthur Robert Dixon
Sidney George Lowe
William Robert Moss
Jack Vernon Thomas Brackenbury
Sidney Arthur Vout.

GREAT YARMOUTH AND GORLESTON

For the famous and historic Norfolk port of Great Yarmouth the flooding on the night of 31 January 1953 was to be a cruel double attack. The first warning of the impending danger was noted about 8.00pm when people crossing the Haven Bridge noticed the angry waters "hissing and foaming" as the waves curved away from the granite buttresses on its way to fill the basin of Breydon Water. People were recorded as being transfixed or "awestruck watching this tremendous wave." A number who saw this phenomena knew it meant trouble, especially when such a force of water attacked the old walls which lined the river Yare and wisely set about warning others and informed the police.

The banks of Breydon Water on the eve of the storm.

Many folks had already left their homes for an evening out at the cinema, The Regal was showing Bing Crosby, Bob Hope and Dorothy Lamour in "*Road to Bali*" with "*Kangaroo Kid*" starring Jock Mahoney as the B film. Shortly after the end of the B film the lights went up in the cinema and the manager stepped in front of the auditorium. His news was serious as he advised anyone who lived over on the other side of Haven bridge to go home because the river was 'very, very high and liable to flooding on Southtown Road.' A number still

One of the high timber carriers of Messrs Jewson helping to evacuate those anxious to leave the Cobholm area.

Above left: A lorry from Garson Blake helps more people evacuate their Cobholm homes.

Above right: A police officer assists in the evacuation of residents by boat and ladder at Cobholm.

Piggy backs and boats evacuated folks from Boreham Road.

decided to stay but many left to make their way home. As they passed over the Haven Bridge many of the returning cinema goers noticed the waters had begun to lap over the banks and quickened their step home to protect what they could of their homes.

Great Yarmouth Borough Police Chief Constable, Mr C F Jelliff, confirmed at the inquest that 'no official warning of the floods was received' but following the rise in water being noticed by beat policemen a loudspeaker car was sent round the danger points at the south end of the town. Here, at Southtown and Cobholm the waters came over first trickling down Steam Mill Lane, Mill Road and into High Mill Road. At 8.45pm the sea had broken over the sea wall and had penetrated Marine Parade. Many homes in the Alderson Road area received the first warnings of impending flood from suspicious gurglings in lavatories and was basins, on inspection householders found water bubbling up and upon looking outside found their drains overflowing. By 8.45pm the area of North Quay between the White Swan and Vauxhall Bridge was almost impassable to cars, water was not spilling over from the sea but rather rising through the drains to over a foot deep! Customers at the White Swan had departed at the first warning and the landlord, Mr Nicholls, had time enough to firmly cork the beer barrels in the cellar and raise his prized piano slightly. Despite being flooded to a depth of four foot Mr Nicholls' quick actions saved many of the pubs assets.

People who had stayed to the end of their films left their cinemas about 10.15pm. Mr Abrey, was 16 at the time and lived on Olive Road, Cobholm, came out of the Regal, he recalled:

"When we comes out the wind was howling, it was raining, really blowing. We goes down the arcade, now there was a lot of panes of glass being smashed with trees. Comes out of the arcade, near the post office and course we could see the waters being blown up in the river from where we comes down. Policeman stops us; were not allowed to go over the bridge, we're supposed to go into the Yare Hotel. So we goes there for a few minutes." Pleading to be let go home because he had his Grandmother and younger brother and sister at home the police let them go. "We gets over Haven Bridge and the water's already over the wall; we're wading through about a foot of water, so we've got our shoes and socks off, our trousers rolled up, and walking through this cold water. As we go past every lamp standard, that's blowing, the water is getting into the electrics so they're sparking up." Eventually getting to their home they are soon joined by their parents who had been at a Beetle Drive at the Windmill Theatre. "…we start lifting some stuff upstairs. And this is a four down, four up house. So we get a lot of stuff lifted up and we're still not flooded out at the time. I suppose we're talking about, half past eleven, twelve o'clock, the whole family go to bed. The next thing we hear is one mighty crash, and there's water everywhere." The banks of Breydon water had finally burst.

Warnings that Breydon had been breached had come as early as 11pm. Many Southtown and Cobholm men had cattle, poultry ponies and horses on the marshes; wives joined their husbands to rescue the animals but by the time they got there the waters were very high. Some, braved the water wading shoulder high but were forced back, their rescues to no

Making the best of it! Taking a row boat out and helping neighbours in Great Yarmouth.

Boats and canoes soon row and paddle along the flooded streets of Cobholm.

avail they returned to defend their homes from the deluge. The electricity supply soon went down plunging the area into an eerie blackness and communications between Cobholm and the outside were lost. When Breydon finally gave way three breaches occurred sending thousands of gallons of water in a 4ft "wall" careering into Cobholm and Southtown. As the water hit the doors and windows of houses were forced in and water swirled into houses. All people could do was people sit tight in their bedrooms as they watched the waters rise outside and saw the carcasses of many of the animals kept on the mashes, their smashed sheds and hen coops drift by. No major rescue attempts were made in this area until Sunday morning.

PC George Baumber and a colleague were patrolling the Yarmouth streets in a police car, they had seen how foul the weather was getting and were not unduly alarmed when the car radio ordered them to warn the people in the local cinemas of the flood danger. A second call sent them to the sea front where boats were in danger of being washed away, in his attempt to secure the boats PC Baumber was washed out. Scrambling back he went home and changed. Returning to duty his attention was drawn by a crowd of people calling for help at Spandler's Yard caravan park on the junction of Exmouth and Barrack Roads. Stripping off his uniform to underwear, but retaining his police helmet to identify him Baumber entered the water. The current in the water was so strong he was almost immediately swept from his feet. Recovering himself he set out again. A member of the police swimming team Baumber swam and waded through the water and debris using the shelter of buildings and walls to the yard where he found the caravans in about 4ft 6" of rising water. In the first caravan he assisted a woman to temporary safety on its roof. In the next he found an 80 year old invalid woman and her son. It was soon apparent it would be impossible to get her out safely he assured the lady of imminent help and making her comfortable he guided her son to safety and the waiting blankets provided by onlookers from Barrack Road.

Returning again to the invalid lady he lifted her to a higher level above the waters. Having been told another woman lived in a further caravan he went there and in danger of crushing from a large stack of wood logs which collapsed before the current he reached the caravan and entered through the widow to find it empty! Baumber left the yard to get a ladder and with some barrels attempted to improvise a raft. Sadly this proved unsuccessful but the invalid lady's son persisted he wanted to rescue his mother. He was a small man and would have stood no chance so Baumber went again, this time swimming just about all the way. Making a higher bed for the woman and providing her with some dry clothes Baumber left her again and went to summon help. He went to telephone for help from the nearby gas works, drenched in water Baumber suffered electric shocks every time he dialled.

Eventually, having worked through the night help arrived at about 6am. Baumber did not leave then he carried on assisting the boat rescues of the people in caravans and others who had clambered onto roofs in the area. For his gallantry PC George Baumber was awarded the British Empire Medal in the Flood Honours.

The signs of danger at Gorleston were noticed as early as 7.30pm when the yachting pond, which is normally about 250 yards from the high water mark, was filled with sea water. At 9pm the sea was level with the breakwater. A tide which was several feet several feet higher than usual was rushing into the harbour mouth and at Brush Quay it was crashing up a slipway opposite the end of Pier Road and flooding the highway. Wave by wave the waters gradually rose above the quay heading and rapidly inundated the low-lying areas of the neighbourhood reaching depths of four or five feet.

When the surge came the timbers to the south of the slipway breached the quay heading, broke up the ancient baulks and scoured out the soil of the quay so that there was a cavity "big enough to put a cottage in." Although most people had realised the howling winds and high waters of the day were abnormal the people of Gorleston, like just about every other flood area of the coast were taken by surprise and their first warning of the disaster came when the water was literally at their doors.

Directly in the path of the breach stood the Belle Vue public house, its landlord, Mr W Burgess said "We were shocked by the way the water rushed in and filled every room to s depth of four feet. It happened so suddenly that in a moment we were up to our waists."

Just a hundred yards away from the Belle Vue was another pub, the King William IV. Its landlord Mr Sam Sykes, a no nonsense former Sheffield butcher and his wife were busy serving customers at about 8.30pm when a customer warned them that the waters were creeping round the back of their house he related what happened next to a *Yarmouth Mercury* reporter: "Half an hour later some customers decided to leave. They opened the front door and the water just rushed in. In next to no time it was above our waists. It cascaded down the stairs leading to our living rooms where it was nearly six feet deep. Just before, a customer, Mr Charles Chilvers, rushed into the kitchen and rescued a dog and two cats which climbed on to the table. Another dog was drowned…The cellar filled up leaving a barrel of beer floating in the passage way leading to the garden where at least ten fowls were drowned in their fowl-houses and other buildings wrecked, Customers trapped in the bar were carried out to higher ground at the bottom of England's Lane."

The experiences of Mr and Mrs G Punchard who lived at the little one story *Mariner's Refuge* at the end of Pier Road is typical of many whose dwellings stood in the immediate path of the flooding sea. At about 8pm Mr and Mrs Punchard had only just ventured out of their beds after being laid up with a bout of 'flu. Rather like the people of the Alderson Road area in Yarmouth they heard a gurgling of water in the sanitary pipes and went outside to investigate the drains. On opening the door they found water lapping round the house and rising fast. Running back in to warn his wife they each grabbed one of their children to take them to safety. Mrs Punchard told a reporter she thought the water had risen to waist height in less than seven minutes. Fighting their way across the road where a neighbour took them in. They had escaped with only the clothes on their backs and their ration books! The next day they were rescued again from the top storey of the house where they had found sanctuary the night before.

The need to provide shelter was uppermost in the minds of the local voluntary medical services. Barely an hour after the sea came over a reception area for evacuees was established. Immediate facilities were provided in the Scout's Hut while the larger St Andrew's Hall was made ready. Initially proposed as simply a shelter many spent their first night of the floods there. On Sunday hot soup was laid on and hot meals followed on the Monday for those still stranded. By this time about 150 people were being provided for by the centre with overflow facilities at Wroughton Junior School.

In the Floral Hall Ballroom a public dance was in full swing when the waters rose. The hall stood on a small knoll slightly higher than Pier Road and its surroundings so it was not until 9.00pm that the manager, Mr R A Micklewright noticed the water creeping towards the steps. Interrupting a waltz he announced to astounded dancers that in view of the storminess of the night and the possibility of flooding that it would be advisable for them to move cars to higher ground. The announcement was greeted by laughter and incredulity but a few people took his advice and shifted their vehicles to the top of Cliff Hill. About an hour later the sea was buffeting the south east segment of the building and the water drawing gradually nearer the main steps. In anticipation of the electricity failing megaphones were got ready and all members of staff issued with candles and brief exactly what to do.

Gorleston quayside the morning after the floods.

Just before 10.30pm when almost completely surrounded by water and with flood water creeping up the entrance steps Mr Micklewright stopped the dance. Many dancers left by the rear entrance by the swimming pool and pushed their way to the cliffs by the high footpath, some went home – others went to the Cliff Hotel and, incredibly, continued dancing. About 60 guests from the outlying villages and towns were marooned in the hall until the small hours when coaches made their way through the abating waters to take their passengers home.

Leading Fireman Fred
Sadd, the hero awarded the
George Medal for his
gallant rescues during the
floods at Gorleston
(*Brian Sadd*)

The first person rescued in Gorleston came about thanks to the dance at the Floral Hall. When the waters had reached Pier Gardens a message came through that there was a gas escape in one of the houses there. It was highly fortunate that the Eastern Gas Board's District Superintendent, Mr J Anderton, was MC at the dance. Arriving at 4 Pier Gardens he discovered Mrs B B Sinclair, a 68-year-old bedridden lady in a front ground floor room with the sheets of her bed floating on the rising waters. Mr Anderton appealed for help and airmen from RAF Hopton who were at the dance backed their liberty wagon up to the house and wading through the water they eased the incapacitated ladys' mattress onto the tail board of their wagon via the window sill. Mrs Sinclair was then removed to the safety of Gorleston vicarage.

It was to be a night of brave rescues and gallantry in Gorleston, the undoubted hero of the town that night – Leading Fireman Fred Sadd. The following is an account of Leading Fireman Sadd's actions compiled from his citation, contemporary news reports and interviews. It started with no hint of the drama that was about to unfold, a call came through to the Gorleston Fire Brigade Sub-Station at ten past ten. Fred answered the call where a very calm sounding voice said "There's a fire at the prefabs in Bells Marsh Road. Apparently there are children involved." The voice crackled and the line went dead.

The four-man relief crew clambered aboard their fire engine and sped off as the gale howled around them. They were not expecting floods so when the engine lurched to a halt Fred thought they were lost, but then he saw the water coming towards them up the street. The whole area was already plunged into blackness by the electricity failure so Fred ordered his appliance to higher ground Pier Plane to survey the scene. There was no fire but it was

Above left: Some of the
prefab houses on Bells
Marsh Road where
Leading Fireman Fred Sadd
waded up to his neck
pulling a boat to rescue
residents (*Brian Sadd*)

Above right: In the distance
Leading Fireman Fred Sadd
begins another long haul
wading through the waters
bringing stranded people to
safety(*Brian Sadd*)

quite clear that the estate consisting of 16 prefab bungalows and some 30 two storey houses was completely flooded to a depth of more than five feet.

A passer by, who proved to be a fisherman, offered the use of a row boat and Sadd, seeing there were several people trapped in the bungalows and houses, and hearing their pitiful cries for help, instructed the fisherman to collect the boat and report back to him with it. Meanwhile, as something approaching panic was reigning in most of the flooded buildings and in the teeth of the gale Sadd and two other men made their way into the flooded district below. Realising the danger and being the tallest man in his crew he sent the other two men back and proceeded alone "I scrambled down about 20ft and started to wade across the flooded gardens. Suddenly I was nearly up to my neck with the soft ground giving under my feet. I could not see any fence tops, ditches or other obstacles until I blundered into them. I shouted to the people in the prefabs to reassure them – though I had not the faintest idea what could be done just then. I waded and swam back to the embankment." The citation enlarges on Fred's modesty: " At times Sadd, who is 6ft 4inches in height and powerfully built, was completely submerged, but although suffering great hardship, by extreme perseverance and courage he alternately waded and swam his way from house to house, greatly reassuring the occupants, and promising them that he would

Leading Fireman Sadd pulls his boat laden with people closer to safety (*Brian Sadd*)

return with a boat to rescue them, and advising them to meanwhile seek refuge at the highest possible point in their dwellings. He then made his way back to high ground."

Fred takes up the story again: "The rowboat was manhandled down the embankment- and I found there were no oars and no bung in the bottom. I filled up the hole with two other men then with the other two men aboard we hoped to overcome the lack of oars by using a piece of wood as a paddle and by pulling the boat along by means of fences." But the force of the wind and flood tide made this impossible. "Time was precious- one of the prefab people had told me that his family could only last out another 15 minutes. We went to him first and saved the man and wife and two little girls." Sadd took them back to the embankment and then continued what he called "a circular tour." He carried two men and a woman to the boat and then a man his wife and a six month old baby in another house.

The boat then became stuck on the top of a garden wall for half an hour. Someone yelled to him that a woman and three children were trapped. Sadd got to them and handed the three babies to another boat, clambered in, took tow of them on his knees and was rowed to dry land. Pulling or pushing his boat as needed Sadd visited each of the

Still having the strength to lift people out of the boat, Leading Fireman Sadd assists the rescued to return to dry land, warm blankets and safety. Those serving with Fred and even the great man himself lost count of how many times he made such journeys during the flood emergency. (*Brian Sadd*)

bungalows. In almost every case, it was impossible to take the boat close up to the bungalows, Sadd therefore had to carry or piggy-back each person in turn from bungalow to boat he rescued numerous men, women and children from the stricken area, including two small girls found floating around their room on a bed. The water was bitterly cold and conditions atrocious, but although suffering severely, Sadd persisted in his efforts.

His citation continues: "After rescuing 5 adults and 5 children in this manner, Sadd collapsed, was given first aid treatment and returned to his station. There he took a shower and changed his clothes and at 03.25 hours on Sunday 1 February, responded to another call in the same location." He had been working for hours, collapsing with exhaustion once and with hardly a break he returned and began pulling boat loads of people to safety again.

When he eventually got home he was too tired to tell his wife what he had done. He slept fitfully, the cramp caused by his long immersion in freezing water and the severe bruising

Leading Fireman Sadd waits at the bottom of the ladder as one of his team assists another person down the ladder to safety. (*Brian Sadd*)

to both legs caused by his countless collisions with obstacles concealed under the water gave him considerable pain. Known initially as "the fireman who swam from window to window" his name was sought by the many who owed their lives to him. His gallantry praised by his watch colleagues the name of Leading Fireman Fred Sadd was soon headline news and even the subject of an "Only the Brave" illustrated story of his gallantry action in the *Eagle* magazine. Fame never went to this modest heros' head and he professed he had only done his duty. Fred Sadd maintained a fine scrap album of his reports but treasured two items above all others; his well earned George Medal and a ten bob note sent anonymously in the letters of appreciation and thanks after his deeds appeared in the newspapers.

The Great Yarmouth and Gorleston Emergency Services control centre that was hastily improvised on the night of the flood. (*Brian Sadd*)

The morning after the flood the nightmare of the night before was lit by the rising sun. The sea had swept in over a wide stretch of marrams smashing up the beach huts at the North End on, rolling to pound the door steps of the guest houses and hotels on the west side of Marine Parade from Jellicoe Road to the Harbours Mouth. The promenade between the Waterways and Britannia Pier had great "bites" taken out of it and its concrete balustrade torn down and the tennis courts and bowling greens of North Drive remained under several feet of water. The most tragic damage on the "Golden Mile" was between Britannia Pier and the Pleasure Beach; Anchor Gardens, the Marina, putting and bowling greens were all still under water. The force of the wall of water was quite clear where it swept in across 150 yards of the Central Beach smashing down the east wall of the bathing pool and a gap torn in the terracing' wreckage, sand and flotsam was strewn everywhere.

The waters in Southtown did not dissipate quickly, especially in the Lichfield, Wolsely and Stafford Road area where three of four feet of water remained for several days and remained impassable to all but those in thigh boots. By the ferry one of the Harbour Commissioners lighters was lifted by the rising tide onto the wharf and left high and dry when the waters subsided, a similar occurrence happened near Jewson's Wharf and the boat was left partly hanging over the edge. Many factories and businesses were badly damaged in the flood along Southtown Road but it did not preclude them helping others if they could.

Despite suffering severe damage to their yard the high timber carriers of Messrs Jewson evacuated a few people who were anxious to leave, row boats and a DUKW joined the evacuation effort during the afternoon and by the evening a steady stream of people were being evacuated from this area.

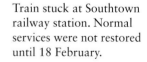

Train stuck at Southtown railway station. Normal services were not restored until 18 February.

Before the flood a small shanty town of caravans, converted buses, bungalows and shacks the existed near railway bridge not far Vauxhall Station. After the flood hardly a sign of its existence remained. The plight of its inhabitants could hardly be imagined. A *Yarmouth Mercury* reporter described the scene:

"the only living things in sight were two pigs, a mother and a youngster that had made their way on to the embankment and stood huddled in the lee of the sleepers lashed by the biting sleet at intervals across Breydon. Shivering parties of homeless people, including many young children , were helpless on the comparatively dry Mill Road. In most cases they had escaped wearing little more than overcoats and it was a pitiful sight to see children, even toddlers standing pathetically by the side of their parents with their naked legs red raw from long exposure to the elements."

At about 9.30am on Sunday morning two policemen arrived at Cobholm. They were the first contact from the town since the previous evenings' deluge. They were to be the first of a steady stream of helpers who brought food, clothing and aid to the stricken area. The water did not subside quickly here, in some areas it remained four of five feet deep. Boats used in the summer for pleasure trips, lorries and vans from local businesses struggled through the water and joined with local emergency services to rescue of stranded people from their bedroom windows. People from all walks of life joined in the rescue effort and there was much talk in the press of "the wartime spirit" of co-operation and triumph through adversity. As men, women, families young and old poured out of the stricken area huddled together aboard lorries they were taken to hastily organised rest centres at the Hospital School, Dene Side Schoolroom and in Rampart Road. Mobile canteens were set up and tickets for meals at restaurants were distributed.

As darkness fell on Sunday rescue operations were considerably hampered by the lack of light and relief was expressed when a DUKW with two portable searchlights aboard was brought into operation. Hundreds of people were still stranded in Cobholm with no hope

Great Yarmouth sea front near the Wintergradens in the aftermath of the floods.

Flood waters still linger around the badly damaged jetty on the Great Yarmouth sea front.

The remains of the jetty, much of its seating destroyed and decking ripped up.

Sand and water carried in to the tennis courts on the sea front, Great Yarmouth.

of rescue until Monday though workers forced their weary bodies to the limit during an all night rescue bid, some had worked for 30 hours when Monday morning came around. Sadly confusion was brought to the rescue attempts as people rescued the previous day were returning in endless steams trying to reach their homes to rescue "just one or two of the things we need."

Following an emergency conference at Great Yarmouth town hall a General Evacuation was ordered and an operation to evacuate as many as 10,000 people was begun at lunchtime on Monday 2 February. The *Yarmouth Mercury* reported:

"...efforts were if anything redoubled in order to clear the area of people before night cast its shadow once more. It was galling to rescuers to fight their way to more remote parts of Cobholm only to find that the few people still remaining had to be practically forced out of their homes. Clinging desperately to a pet cat or a treasured ornament old ladies were carried bodily through the flood and dumped without ceremony onto lorries. In Stone Road and Breydon Terrace, still flooded to a depth of over five feet, people were peering

Filling sandbags and building a protective wall at the Marina open air theatre, Great Yarmouth.

Clearing up some of the detritus of the flood from the waters of the quay.

Displaced wooden bricks and flood waters linger on the quayside at Great Yarmouth.

Cars and lorries make their way through the flood waters at the Cobholm end of Southtown Road during the morning after the deluge.

from bedrooms at 4.00pm. Broadcast appeals and even threats seemed to have no effect and in the end it was only by telling them their water supplies would be cut off and no food would be brought out to them that one or two people could be got out."

Evacuated people, from across Great Yarmouth were taken to the Gorleston and Caister holiday camps, there had been little time to prepare these centres and many of the camp hutments were for summer use only and not heated; oil heaters were provided and a fire engine despatched to stand by at the camp. Confusion reigned for many hours in spite of the tireless efforts of the Civil Defence, St John Ambulance and camp helpers. Distraught women wandered through the camp seeking the rest of their families from whom they had been separated whilst in the hurriedly improvised nursing room dozens of cuts and bruises received attention. One St John nurse related "In the lounges people sat as in a dream, staring before them, unable to comprehend what had happened to them. If spoken to they did not answer and were apparently unaware that there were others in the same plight all round them. One or two younger men and women were striving to forget their troubles

As the flood waters abated so began the massive task of pumping out the remaining flood water, drying out houses and for returning householders to see what could be salvaged among their furniture and effects.

and were aiding the very old and very young. Occasionally two people would stare at each other and then, realising that the person they were looking at was a close relative they would break into voluble greetings."

On the afternoon of Wednesday 4 February the inquest into the Yarmouth flood victims was convened by Borough Coroner Mr G L Talbot. The deaths of seven victims were discussed, namely Mrs Rose Rebecca Monson (76) of 8 and Mrs Lucy May Ward (61) of 17 Bridge Road, Runham Vauxhall; Miss Lilian Ruth Fox-Cautman (63) of 64 Albany Road, Miss Martha Elizabeth Everitt (84) of 114 Wolseley Road; Mr Ronald William Parmenter (24) of 31 Dene Side, Mrs Sarah Milligan (87) of 1 Exmouth Square and Miss Ethel Alice Brown (73) of 4 Monarch Terrace, Exmouth Road. At the time of this inquest the other two victims could not be discussed:- The body of Miss Doris May Talbot (39) was only found at 195 Stafford Road on the afternoon of the inquest . The body of Mrs Rose Nimmon (70) of Trivett's Level, Cobholm who was swept away had still not been recovered.

Harrowing stories were told at the inquest. The landlord of the Vauxhall Gardens pub gave evidence and described how 61 year old Mrs Lucy Ward had waded to his pub in 4ft of water at 11.40pm with her dog. At 12.10 am, insisting she wanted to return home despite the fast flowing water swirling by the pub she was advised to keep hold of the railings to stop her getting carried off by the waters. At 12.20am the dog came back to the pub and cried at the door. Police

Sgt J Burniston then described finding Mrs Ward's body at the junction of Acle and Bridge Roads, against the old tollhouse where it had been carried by the water.

Ernest Harbord then gave evidence that his mother in law, 87 year old Mrs Sarah Milligan was being looked after by one of her daughters, Mrs Hunt, from Lowestoft on the Saturday night. When the water began to enter the house at about 10pm Mrs Hunt told her mother she must go upstairs. Mrs Milligan , who was very unwell, adamantly refused and clung on to her bed so she could not be moved manually. As the water rose Mrs Hunt managed to drag her to the stairs, but the weight of the water gradually dragged Mrs Milligan back down. Laurence Sidney Scott of 110 Palgrave Road described going to the house by boat and finding Mrs Milligan and her daughter at the bottom of the stairs. Dr Noreen Evans a house surgeon at Yarmouth General Hospital stated Mrs Milligan died in the hospital from shock.

Frederick Jarrold of 79 Exmouth Road stated 73 year old Mrs Ethel Brown died at his home after he had rescued her from her home on Saturday night, he had discovered her completely submerged, entangled in an iron bedstead.

The death of Ronald Parmenter (24), the youngest victim at Yarmouth, was described by Mrs Maisie Rose Martin of Exmouth Road. Watching the floods from her bedroom window she saw a young man at the corner of the road at 1.40pm on Sunday. He was described as appearing to hesitate and seemed to speak to someone and then crossed the road, the water nearly up to his thigh boots. He walked along holding the fence then his face seemed to grimace in pain. Half turning he fell face down in the water. Mrs Martin and her father blew a whistle and called for help until two men came. One of the men, Walter Harvey of 20 Ordnance Road said they pulled Parmenter out and tried to pump the water out of him but sadly the young man died.

Other victims of the flood were found in water in their own homes, one of them, Miss Everitt was discovered by PC Houghton who had to relate she was found face down in just four or five inches of water. The verdict on all seven victims recorded at the inquest was "Death by misadventure."

The small boat rescues and evacuations removed hundreds form their homes in Yarmouth and Gorleston.

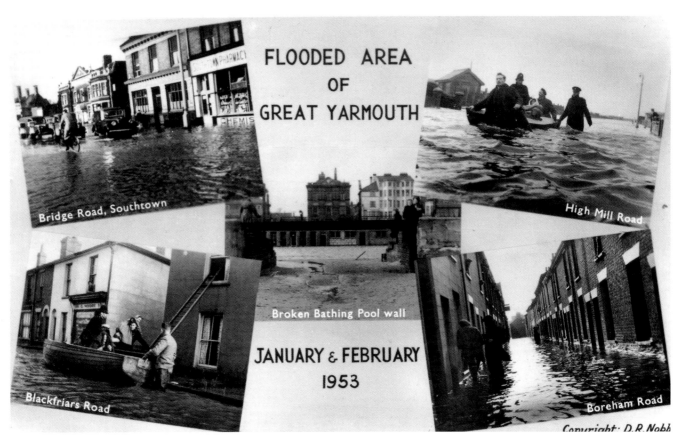

The two multi-view postcards of the 1953 floods at Great Yarmouth by local photographer D. R. Nobbs

AFTERMATH

When dawn came on the morning of Sunday 1 February 1953 the east coast of England was an appalling sight. RAF aircrews who sent were sent out at first light on aerial reconnaissance over the damaged areas in 'Operation Floodlight' saw the full horror of the previous night's invasion by sea and storm. Sea defences had been breached along three quarters of the east coast and thousands of acres of land were now under water. Many of the streets of the county ports and coastal towns, normally dotted with vehicles and activity, were eerily empty. As crews flew over they noted how the sun caught these rivers, which were formerly streets and roads and how these waters seemed to glisten unnaturally in the early morning light. What were previously railway goods yards and docks had become large expanses of water obstructed by occasional signal boxes and cranes. The county just didn't look right. As one pilot recalled 'maps were almost out of the window.' The bank between King's Lynn and Hunstanton, usually marked by its white painted bungalow settlements and beach huts was reduced to a sodden mass of splintered wood, with what building and boats that did survive left lying around like toys. Villages like Cley and Salthouse, normally distanced from the sea by salt marsh and embankments were new waterside settlements. The cliffs of north-east Norfolk were now observed to be punctuated by a number of new shallow bays, carved out by the sea when the water had smashed into them.

Over the ensuing weeks the extent of loss and damage caused by flood and storm became apparent and was collated from across the eastern counties to reveal a death toll of 307. There were 24,500 houses damaged, 47,500 home without an electricity supply, 200 industrial premises out of action and over 150,000 acres of land rendered sterile for a year or more and thousands of farm animals drowned. I had been a provident thing that these statistics were not known in the immediate aftermath of the disaster – for those on the front line of the floods the devastation and suffering that confronted them was quite enough to deal with at the time.

The relief effort that began on the night of the disaster was truly outstanding. The voluntary medical organisations such as the St John Ambulance, British Red Cross Society and even the RSPCA were at the forefront of rescues with civil and military services, while the WVS (Women's Voluntary Service) were straight in with the welfare support. Ladies like Mrs. Darbyshire-Bowles, who, living at Old Catton at the time, responded to the call for blankets at 11.00pm. Driving her W.V.S. van, loaded with Blankets and stores, complete with tea urn and two volunteers picked up on the way. Through the howling gale, roads littered with branches and debris and even avoiding a flying haystack, they eventually

Mr. and Mrs. G. Clarke who were rescued by the police at 3.30am on the morning of 1 February 1953 from the Coastguard Cottages just 50 yards from the beach at Sea Palling. Their first concern on the morning they were photographed was the going down of the second tide and their chickens which they had found safe and sound behind the sea wall! (John Clarke)

Local fire pumps and appliances joined by those of the Lancashire County Fire Service during the 96-hour continuous pumping operation after the deluge to get the remaining flood waters into a manageable state. (*Gressenhall Farm and Workhouse Museum of Norfolk Life*)

Queue for the relief centre
at the Southtown Drill Hall,
Great Yarmouth.

arrived to attend to the needs of the people at Heacham, Snettisham and Hunstanton. They
were all unstinting in their efforts, some working twenty or thirty hour shifts from their
first call-out.

By the night of Sunday 1 February a Food Flying Squad consisting of about 35 members
of the WVS and Civil Defence Corps, consisting of four canteens, one food stores van, one
camp stores van, one water tanker, one motor cycle and one utility van was despatched
from Cambridge to King's Lynn to help feed the homeless (a service they carried out until
5 February when their work was taken over by British and American military static
kitchens.) In the Cley area the WVS organised a meals on wheels round for older people
in their own homes if they were without cooking facilities and unable to get to the
community centre for meals. Donations of food came thick and fast from members of the
public, businesses from across the UK and the Ministry of Food. Donations were
unpacked, shared out and repacked into individual parcels by WVS volunteers. Distribution
was rapid: for example the British Red Cross and WVS worked together in Great Yarmouth
to dispense 4,000 parcels in two days.

Realising from previous experience the next demand after food would be clothing the
WVS alerted all its clothing officers immediately. Fortunately the WVS had appealed for
clothing in the autumn of 1952 so that it might be prepared to meet just such an emergency
as this. Stocks were held locally, enabling the WVS to meet the needs of thousands of people
on the spot. In King's Lynn, 4,200 garments were issued in the first two days. Over the
ensuing weeks national and local initiatives and collection centres for donated clothes were
established to maintain supplies. In Great Yarmouth alone the WVS ladies aided by
volunteers from The St John Ambulance Brigade and British Red Cross Society distributed
a quarter of a million garments to 20,000 people. Over the following weeks and months
gifts of food, clothes, comforts and equipment were received from clubs, associations,
businesses and countries from all over the world including Greece, Canada, America and
even Ethiopia. Furniture and carpets were sent by lorry load from all over Britain for
distribution by voluntary services to those who had lost their in the flood (the work of

Round Table was particularly notable in this part of the flood relief effort).

The first dignitary to see the disaster for herself was the Queen, who had been staying at Sandringham at the time. Some of her own estate had been deluged by waters. Accompanied by the Duke of Edinburgh and the Duke of Gloucester she embarked on a tour of the flood ravaged areas of West Norfolk on Monday 2 February. Beginning their journey at King's Lynn the visibly concerned Royal party, accompanied by the Mayor Mr Claude Freestone, the Town Clerk and Police Superintendent Fred Calvert, saw the worst hits areas of the town for themselves, spoke to rescue workers and visited the Gaywood Park Secondary School, a rest centre for 700 people. For a short while children forgot their worries and sung nursery rhymes to the Queen who later spent time meeting some of the people evacuated to the centre. Her demeanour was unhurried and she listened intently to the harrowing stories that unfolded.

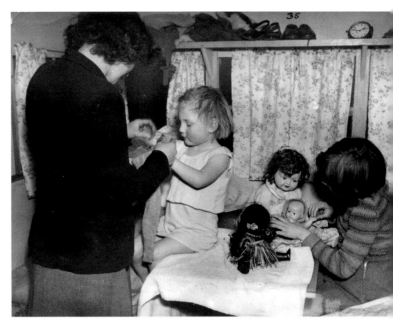

Mrs Jack Cook and her two children Susan and Sheila settle into their temporary home in a caravan, 6 February 1953. They had been stranded in their Salthouse cottage, which had partially collapsed, until 1.00am on Sunday 1 February when they were able to wade to safety.

In the afternoon the Royal party went to Hunstanton. The first stop was the relief headquarters at the Sandringham Hotel where she stopped and spoke to some of the American Servicemen's wives who were helping to feed the rescue workers on South Beach Road. Joined by an entourage of civil and military officials the Royal party was taken to see the South Beach Road area where the rescue efforts were still in progress. It was here Her Majesty was told the story of the brave deeds performed by Airman Reis Leming of the USAAF who had rescued many in the teeth of the storm on that fateful night. Over the following weeks many dignitaries including Harold Macmillan and Mrs Clementine Churchill, wife of Prime Minister Winston Churchill followed in the footsteps of the Queen visiting disaster sites along the Norfolk coast.

As the waters abated the British and American military along with local council workers and volunteers did an outstanding job clearing up displaced wooden buildings, buried cars, large items of debris and detritus left behind as well as rebuilding seas defences in the bitterly cold weather. As the clean-up effort progressed fire engines and pumps were sent from all over England to help pump out the flooded towns along the coast. Backed up by

Volunteers of all ages help clear up the debris of trees broken by the flood at Abraham's Bosom, Wells-next-the-Sea, February 1953.

Clearing the Salthouse to Cley Road of sand on 4 January 1953. (*Gressenhall Farm and Workhouse Museum of Norfolk Life*)

Sir Rupert de la Bère, The Lord Mayor of London (second left) with local dignitaries and residents, at the St John Hall, Cley, during his official visit to North Norfolk in August 1953. He came to see the progress of the flood relief work for himself and learn how the Lord Mayor's Fund had helped victims of the floods.

voluntary organisations and military canteens they were kept supplied with millions of cups of tea, hot soup and sandwiches to 'keep 'em going.' In the space of about two weeks and with no little thanks to tireless work by many hands, most of the evacuated people had returned to their homes.

Householders returned to find the floors of their homes covered in a horrible slimy, stinky filled mud filled with all manner of detritus from the sea and flood wreckage mixed up with treasured possessions, provisions, crockery and furniture most of which was found to be beyond salvage. Some houses were found to be more pungent than others having several dead fish left behind, some people were even unfortunate enough to find a dead farm animal that had been washed in and had lain undetected in the hallway. Great Yarmouth's Medical Officer of Health advised householders that it was not necessary to use disinfectants in cleaning houses after the floods. He stated 'The policy of general cleanliness...no one is going to get a disease unless they get the water into their mouths.'

In many areas the military stepped in again and loaned people large dryers and many companies donated large amounts of coal and solid fuel to speed up the drying out process. Despite the good will the effect of the salt soaking into walls was almost permanent so many houses ended up with their ground floors being plaster boarded throughout. Even today houses without this protection show the tell-tale brown stain within days of redecoration. Insurance claims from the 24,000 damaged homes across the eastern counties totalled in excess of £1½ million – an average of about £60 per home.

To help ease the situation a number of fund-raising schemes and relief initiatives were undertaken both locally and nationally. The Lord Mayor of London's National Flood and Tempest Distress Fund was endowed with millions from the public and enhanced by government contributions. The notion of this scheme was to avoid bureaucracy; the Mayor's Fund would handle payment of compensation while the government would meet the costs of emergency repairs, the reinstatement of seas defences and the restoration of agricultural land. In 1973 the fund was still paying £26,000 annually to the surviving dependents of flood victims. In Norfolk a County Relief Fund was established within days of the disaster, headed by Lord Lieutenant Edmund Bacon and endorsed by a gallery of civic leaders. Within days of the announcement in the newspapers many local people and businesses had dug deep and raised thousands.

Slowly but surely the storm wrecked coastal residents of Norfolk and the rest of the Eastern Counties began to rebuild their lives and their homes but they would never forget the night of 'the '53 floods.' Everyone prays they will never see another night like it and much time is still spend debating and enacting worthwhile sea defence schemes, but in the concluding words of the Dereham Coroner, Mr. L. R. Allwood, spoken after an inquest into victims of the flood: 'We are an island nation surrounded by the sea, man cannot control nature...and quite certainly England cannot be girt by concrete walls.'

Members of the River Board inspecting the repairs and remaining flood damage at Salthouse, May 1955. Behind them is Randall's Folly an historic building sadly damaged beyond repair by the floods and which had to be demolished.

AWARDS FOR GALLANTRY AND SERVICES PERFORMED DURING THE EAST COAST FLOODS 1953

THE GEORGE MEDAL
Staff Sergeant Freeman A. Kilpatrick USAAF (Hunstanton)
Airman 3rd Class Reis Leming USAAF (Hunstanton)
Leading Fireman Fred Sadd (Gorleston)

Frederick Beckerton holds his son Peter's posthumous Albert Medal and his wife Vera with her BEM after their presentation at Buckingham Palace, 1953 (*Hazel Bolton*)

THE ALBERT MEDAL
Mr. Peter Beckerton (Snettisham)

ST. JOHN AMBULANCE LIFE SAVING MEDAL (SILVER CLASS)
Supt. Leslie Eaton, St John Ambulance Brigade (Wells-next-the-Sea)

MEMBER, THE MOST EXCELLENT ORDER OF THE BRITISH EMPIRE (MBE)
Supt. Fred Calvert, Norfolk Constabulary (King's Lynn)
Supt. William Garner, Norfolk Constabulary (Sea Palling)
Commandant Miss Helen Barclay, British Red Cross Society (Wiveton)

THE BRITISH EMPIRE MEDAL (BEM)
Detective Inspector G. F. F. Daniels, Norfolk Constabulary (King's Lynn)
Sub Officer Sidney Lancaster, Norfolk Fire Brigade (Sea Palling)
Asst. Divisional Officer R. L. Pearson, Norfolk Fire Brigade
Divisional Supt. R. William Smith, St John Ambulance Brigade (Hunstanton)
Divisional Supt. A. E. Stringer, St John Ambulance Brigade (King's Lynn)
Divisional Supt. A. V. Croote, St John Ambulance Brigade (South Lynn)
Div. Officer B. W. Elsden, St John Ambulance Brigade (Salthouse)
Police Sergeant Gerald Bunney, Norfolk Constabulary (Snettisham)
PC Henry Nobbs, Norfolk Constabulary (Snettisham)
PC G. W. Baumber, Norfolk Constabulary (Great Yarmouth)
Firewoman Jean Belding (King's Lynn)
Harbour Master Frank Smith (Wells-next – the-Sea)
Mr. G. S. Drewery, Motor Vehicle Fitter, British Road Services (Snettisham)
Mrs. Vera Beckerton (Snettisham)

QUEEN'S COMMENDATION FOR BRAVE CONDUCT

Station Officer John Fleming, Norfolk Fire Brigade (Hunstanton)
Divisional Supt. John Briggs, St John Ambulance Brigade (Salthouse and Cley)
Commandant Kathleen Bloomfield, British Red Cross Society (Cley)
PC Noel Donne, Norfolk Constabulary (King's Lynn)
PC Raymond Skerritt, Norfolk Constabulary (King's Lynn)
Electricity Sub Station Attendant Charles Skipper (King's Lynn)
George Jay (Wells-next-the-Sea)
Frederick Ellender (Wells-next-the-Sea)
Arthur Cook (Sea Palling)
Arthur Mason (Sea Palling)
Geoffrey Searle (Hunstanton)
William Stoney (Hunstanton)

Note: The place names show in brackets in the above roll state the place where the recognised action or service was performed.

Divisional Superintendents A.E. Stringer BEM and A. V. Croote BEM of King's Lynn (far left) join other St John Ambulance flood award recipients (left to right) Area Commissioner R. C. Hannant (Great Yarmouth & Gorleston), Mrs. J.H. Yull (County Secretary), Lady Cook, Sir Thomas Cook, Divisional Superintendent R.W. Smith BEM (Hunstanton), Divisional Superintendent J. T. Briggs and Divisional Officer B. W. Elsden BEM (Holt) at the Buckingham Palace investiture on 10 July 1953.

R.S.P.C.A. AWARDS FOR GALLANTRY AND SERVICES ON BEHALF OF ANIMALS DURING THE EAST COAST FLOODS 1953

NORWICH AREA

R.S.P.C.A. GALLANTRY MEDAL:
Mrs. M. O. French (Wells)
Mr. W. E. Cooper (Wells-next-the-Sea)
Mr. C. Cox (Wells-next-the-Sea)
Mr. T. Jordan (Wells-next-the-Sea)
Mr. J. Fairbrother (Wells-next-the-Sea)
Mr. J. Cox (Wells-next-the-Sea)
R.S.P.C.A. Inspector J. McCluskey (Norwich)
R.S.P.C.A. Inspector H. J. Guyton (East Dereham)
R.S.P.C.A. Senior Inspector E. C. Green (Thetford)
S.Sgt. J. J. Belcher (47th Maintenance Squadron, USAAF Sculthorpe)

GREAT YARMOUTH AREA

R.S.P.C.A. GALLANTRY MEDAL:
Mr. D. Pitcher (Caister-on-Sea)
Mr. G. Daniels (Hemsby)
Mr. R. J. Tooley (Great Yarmouth)
Mr. P. Ellett (Great Yarmouth)
Mr. R. Yaxley (Great Yarmouth)
Mr. S. Parsley (Great Yarmouth)
Mr. R. Brewer (Great Yarmouth)
Mr. W. Beckett (Great Yarmouth)
R.S.P.C.A. Inspector L. C. Tye (Great Yarmouth)
Mr. A. Benjafield (Great Yarmouth)

R.S.P.C.A. Meritorious Service Medal
Mrs. D. Tye (Great Yarmouth)
Miss P. Tye (Great Yarmouth)
Mrs. R. Wood (Great Yarmouth)
Mr. A. Browne (Great Yarmouth)

Acknowledgements

THE AUTHOR WOULD like to express his thanks to all those who have so kindly contributed to and encouraged this book. I am particularly indebted to those who shared their often harrowing personal memories of the 1953 floods with me; my thanks, respect and admiration go especially to them. I am also indebted to Gressenhall Farm and Workhouse Museum of Norfolk Life for the use of their archives and a number of their pictures. I would also like to extend a particular thanks to the following:

Mr and Mrs Reis Leming GM; Debra Ross; Brian Sadd; Hazel and Jack Bolton; Ronald Meek; David Bocking; all the helpful staff at the Norfolk Heritage Centre, Norfolk & Norwich Millennium Library; Judy Bates and Mike Last at the *Lynn News*; East Midland Allied Press Ltd; BBC Radio Norfolk; Mrs. Maureen Sayer; Terence Dalton Ltd., Lavenham, Suffolk; Ann Meakin and the members of Martham Local History Group; Thomas Cook Esq; Tony Framingham; Kitty Lynn; Mr and Mrs Neil Quincey; Mrs Joan Mayne; Norfolk Constabulary Archives; Norfolk Museums and Archaeology Service; Steve Snelling; Keith Skipper; John Clarke; Robin Driscoll; Roger Kingstone; Sheila Flynn; Michael Sismey; Simon Butler and Sharon O'Inn at Halsgrove Publishing; Wendy Elsden; Dick Meadows, Terry Burchell for much of the original photographic work for the 1953 floods chapter; the late Leslie and Barbara Eaton and the late Harold Cooke.

I would like to record particular thanks to Mike Wilson for his kind permission to quote from the interviews he and his team from Masque Theatre recorded, transcribed and originally published in *Wall of Water* and to Paul Randell for the kind loan of the Roy Randell album and for permission to reproduce the Roy Randell letter.

Every attempt has been made to acknowledge copyright for the images used in this book, the majority of them are from originals in the author's collection or credited as appropriate. If there are any omissions or errors please accept my respectful apologies: no attempt to infringe rights was intended.

The floods at Salthouse, 1938.

Select Bibliography

Books

Butcher, Brian *A Movable and Rambling Police* (Norwich 1989)

Dalton, Nell and Ebdon, Paul (eds.) *A Wall of Water* (Fakenham, Norfolk 1985)

Goose, Herbert Howell *Norwich Under the Water* (Norwich 1912)

Harland, M.G. and Harland H.J. *The Flooding of Eastern England* (Peterborough, 1980)

Ogley, Bob, Davison, Mark and Currie, Ian *The Norfolk and Suffolk Weather Book* (Kent 1993)

Pollard, Michael *North Sea Surge* (Lavenham, Suffolk, 1985)

Purchas, Arthur W., *Some History of Wells Next the Sea & District* (Ipswich 1965)

Roberts & Co, *City of Norwich Illustrated Record of the Great Flood of August 1912* (Norwich 1912)

Summers, Dorothy *The East Coast Floods* (Newton Abbot, 1978)

Storey, Neil R. *Flood Alert – Norfolk 1953* (Stroud, Gloucestershire 2003)

Tooke, Colin *Great Yarmouth and Gorleston: The Floods 1953* (Caister, Norfolk 2002)

Reports, Journals and Official Publications:

Conference on The North Sea Floods of 31 January/1 February, 1953: A Collection of Papers Presented at the Institution in December 1953 The Institution of Civil Engineers, London 1954

Mill, Hugh Robert, *Unprecedented Rainfall in East Anglia, August 25-26, 1912* Quarterly Journal of the Royal Meteorological Society Vol. XXXIX No. 165 (January 1913)

Mosby, J.E.G. *The Horsey Flood, 1938: An Example of Storm Effect on a Low Coast* The Geographical Journal Vol. 93, No. 5, May 1939 pp. 413 -418

National Rivers Authority (Anglia Region*), The 1953 East Coast Floods: The Battle to Prevent it Happening Again* (1993)

Report on the WVS Work in the East Coast Flood Disaster 1953 (London 1953)

The Norfolk Sea Floods February 1938 in *Transactions of the Norfolk and Norwich Naturalists' Society* Vol. XIV., Part IV., 1938

Newspapers and Magazines

Daily Express
Daily Herald
Daily Mirror
Dereham & Fakenham Times
East Anglian Daily Times
East Anglian Magazine
Eastern Daily Press
Illustrated London News
London Gazette
Lynn News
Norfolk Fair
Norfolk Chronicle
St John Ambulance Review
The Times
Wisbech Advertiser
Yarmouth Mercury